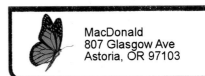
THE
SECRET
GARDEN:

GROWING DELICIOUS FOOD FOR

ESSENTIAL
LIVING

D1023170

ALTERNATIVE
DAILY

This page intentionally left blank.

This page intentionally left blank.

It's Time to Get Your Hands Dirty

I remember as a child working in my grandparents' little country market in the middle-of-nowhere, Iowa. People would come for miles to partake in the sweet aroma of warm tomatoes and taste the crispness of fresh corn on the cob.

My hardworking grandmother would haul-in baskets of produce from the field and display it like a treasure. By the day's end, there would be little left of the harvest apart from the share my grandparents would keep for supper.

Cucumbers, melons, tomatoes, corn, cabbage, potatoes, onions, carrots and peppers were staples when I visited my grandparents. They took immense pride in their beautiful produce — fresh, organic and very real! Their hands were blistered, their brows glistened but they were happy. Happy for what the land provided, happy to work for their food and share it with others.

This is where my love of gardening started. I would help my grandparents gingerly pluck tomatoes from the vine. They were warm in my little hands and oh-so-beautiful. There was something so special about eating this earthy food full of sweet natural goodness. From the time I was very small, I knew the value of getting my hands dirty. I knew I was destined to be a gardener.

Fast forward many years, my children are grown and I reflect on the many gardens we have had. The hours spent cultivating the land, building raised beds and teaching my children the value of home-grown food. Through the sweat, blisters and dirt, they have all developed an appreciation of what hard work yields and how to work with the land to grow food.

Now, more than ever, it is important to learn the skills associated with growing food and to share these with the generations to come. We live in very uncertain times, and our food supply is extremely fragile and unhealthy. If you are in search of the security that growing your own food brings, now is the time. If you want the healthiest option for you and your family, now is the time.

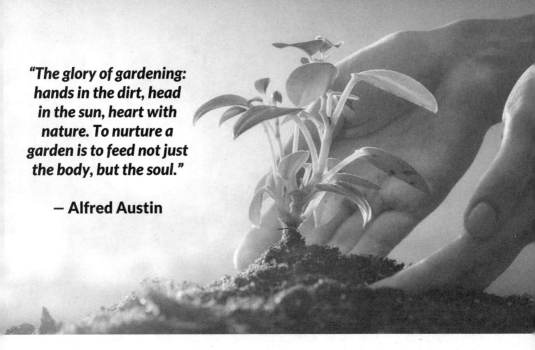

"The glory of gardening: hands in the dirt, head in the sun, heart with nature. To nurture a garden is to feed not just the body, but the soul."

— Alfred Austin

This book is meant for those just starting out on their growing journey, for those hungry to be self-sufficient, and for those who are seasoned gardeners looking for an overall great reference guide to growing food.

I dedicate this book to my three girls who have been gardening with me for more than 20 years. May the dirt on your hands be a reminder of the countless gardens we have sowed together.

Enjoy your journey to a better tomorrow. Now is the time to get your hands dirty!

Susan Patterson,
Certified Master Gardener

This page intentionally left blank.

Table of Contents

A Brief History of the American Garden: Growing Food at Home

In the early pioneering days of America, most people grew their own food, learning how to cultivate and grow it with the help of Native Americans — a home garden was necessary for survival. In the 17th-century, those settlers farmed their own fruits and vegetables, often using small, enclosed gardens that sat just outside their front door. Typically these gardens were focused on essential edibles, culinary and medicinal herbs.

While food gardening has waxed and waned since then, it will never stop. In fact, in recent years it has become increasingly popular, with an estimated 35% of American households currently growing food at home or in a community garden — a number that's increased by 17% in just five years. Younger households have seen significant increases in recent years, skyrocketing 63% to 13 million over the last decade, according to the National Gardening Association.

I'm happy to be a part of those numbers and hope that those figures continue to increase. It is also fascinating to see just how much gardening has evolved.

Early 19th Century

As America entered the 1800s, settlers were continuing to move west, and most people focused on sustenance. They used kitchen gardens that grew close to their backdoors which made them easy to protect, maintain and harvest. The sites would either be totally flat, slightly raised or pitched to encourage drain-off, and they were most often entirely enclosed by fencing.

Instead of colorful flowers, gardens included what was needed for survival: food and medicinal plants, with fruit trees, vegetables and herbs prevailing. In addition to food, gardens provided medicine, dyes, fragrances and aromatic herbs for the home. Pioneers dried their fruits and herbs while preserving and pickling fruits and veggies to ensure nutrition all year round. They would hang their herbs to dry, with onions and peppers often hung in wreaths or braids.

Arguably the best-known gardener from the early colonial days was Thomas Jefferson. Gardening was his passion. He collected varieties of vegetables from across the globe; he bred and tested them, before selecting the very best for seed-saving. He also kept incredibly detailed reports of his gardening experiments (more on this to come).

Mid-19th Century

As the years went by, gardening became more of a leisure activity as towns grew and public markets appeared. Ornamental gardens became all the rage, with plant breeders focusing on new garden varieties while researchers worked on addressing plant pests and diseases. Tools were designed for fighting pests, like pyrethrum (dried, crumbled chrysanthemum flower heads), which were imported for protection. Extracts from these flower heads are still used. In fact, they are the active ingredient in some of the most powerful natural pesticides available today.

Late 19th Century

Just before the turn of the century, home gardens were moved to backyards, with the former front-door gardens replaced by manicured lawns and exotic flowers. Gardens that were once meant for public viewing, now often included "hidden" gardens in private areas, protected and out of the public eye.

Early 20th Century

Gardens continued to be all about the "look" as interest in edible gardening waned, with more Americans moving to urban areas with the increase in manufacturing jobs. The "in" thing was for American garden designers to create more natural looking gardens using native plants that were once considered too weed-like, rather than nursery-cultivated varieties. Many home gardens adopted the new garden styles from England. These included elaborate beds of perennials and larger lawns framed by massive shrubs, with foundation plantings grown near the home.

Victory gardens, originally called "liberty gardens" or "war gardens," made their first appearance during World War I. President Woodrow Wilson called on Americans to plant vegetable gardens to ward off the possible threat of food shortages. Many took up the challenge as a civic and patriotic duty. Front yards, backyards, vacant lots and even schoolyards were turned into vegetable gardens. President Woodrow Wilson and First Lady Edith decided to use sheep, who grazed and fertilized the lawns at the White House in an effort to save on fuel, chemicals and human labor. America became the world's leading seed supplier during this period as Europe faced mounting seed shortages.

The 1940s

Things ramped up even more with the advent of World War II, which is considered a game-changer in the history of vegetable gardens. People were urged to grow as much of their own food as they could in order to help the war effort, and the victory garden became an even greater symbol of patriotism and self-reliance. In 1943, President Franklin D. Roosevelt and First Lady Eleanor planted a victory garden on the grounds of the White House. By this time, there were some 20 million victory gardens throughout the United States, supplying over 40 percent of all American produce grown that year. But as the war ended, interest in orchards and vegetable gardens began to fade.

After the war, the U.S. chemical factories that had been producing nitrogen for bombs needed to make money another way, so they began marketing nitrogen as a fertilizer for farms. This gave birth to chemical farming and vegetable gardening, and it was also the beginning of environmental degradation.

Mid-20th Century

Post-war technology helped to simplify gardening and improve success, with products like Sevin insecticide and Daconil fungicide used to fight pests and disease. As pesticides were used more and more extensively, people were beginning to see the consequences in dead birds and other animals that were obvious casualties of spraying. Rachel Carson published *Silent Spring* in 1962, warning of the consequences of the detrimental effects of these products. She was met with fierce opposition, including personal attacks and lawsuits from chemical companies, including Monsanto. Despite that, then-president John F. Kennedy requested an investigation into her claims, which lead to better regulation of pesticides.

The 1970s and 1980s

Things started to turn again in 1970, first with the creation of Earth Day signaling a renewed interest in growing food at home. Garden designers began including fruits and vegetables in with the ornamentals in formal designs, and edible landscaping started to become popular. School-based community gardens increased, energized by concerns about the environment and urban revitalization, allowing students to absorb science while spending time outdoors and discovering the delights of fresh-grown vegetables. Urban community gardens and organic gardening became more widespread as well.

The following decade saw the term "xeriscape" come into use, coined for landscapes in dry climates which were filled with water-wise plants. Drought-tolerant, low-maintenance plants were used more prominently and gardens became an extension of the home rather than separate areas.

The 1990s Through Today

The 1990s introduced a new trend of small space gardening, with urban populations growing at the fastest rate in U.S. history. Those with small urban spaces began to use containers, trellises and permanent planters built into hardscapes. The Clintons hoped to bring vegetable gardening back to the White House but were denied due to the formal nature of the grounds. Eventually, it was allowed, but only on a hidden spot on the roof of the White House. It wasn't until 2009 that the Obamas were able to change all that with the largest White House vegetable garden to date established right on the south lawn.

The turn of the millennium saw edible gardens come into vogue once again with the desire for more fresh, organic local foods. By 2013, a third of all American households reported growing their own food.

I am happy to report that the desire to grow food seems to be alive and well in millions of American homes, big and small. Organic gardening is leading the way with more and more people committed to their health and the health of the environment.

Sustainable food: it's something that has changed my life, and I hope that if you already have not experienced it, it will change yours as well.

"Everything that slows us down and forces patience,
everything that sets us back into the slow circles of nature, is a help.
Gardening is an instrument of grace."

— May Sarton

What Thomas Jefferson Taught Me About Gardening

"No occupation is so delightful to me as the culture of the earth, and no culture comparable to that of the garden... But though an old man, I am but a young gardener."

— Thomas Jefferson, 1811

When you think of Thomas Jefferson, you probably equate him with the term "founding father," but Jefferson was also a passionate gardener and a true trailblazer in gardening practices. He wasn't just a pioneer of our nation, but a crop scientist. His Monticello garden was a Revolutionary American garden that is believed to have first been inspired during a trip to England on business with good friend John Adams. During the pair's two-month stay, they toured English gardens and observed how they grew.

When Jefferson retired from public life, moving into the hilltop plantation in Virginia, his garden became somewhat of an "experimental testing lab," said Monticello's head gardener and author of *A Rich Spot of Earth* Peter Hatch. He said, "This was where he'd try new vegetables that he'd sought out from around the globe." The signer of the Declaration of Independence culled from virtually every western culture known at the time, growing the earth's melting pot of immigrant vegetables.

In a letter to Charles W. Peale in 1811, Jefferson wrote, "No occupation is so delightful to me as the culture of the earth, and no culture comparable to that of the garden... But though an old man, I am but a young gardener."

At Monticello, he truly became a pioneer of gardening practices that are useful for us today. Those dutiful, detailed observations became the basis for his extensive gardening ideas that still influence us today. And, I can honestly say that though he's been gone for centuries now, Jefferson significantly influenced my life when it comes to food and gardening.

How?

Experimentation

Jefferson certainly wasn't one to limit himself to only popular garden staples. He grew 17 different varieties of fruits and 330 different varieties of vegetables at Monticello. He inspired me to plant a wide range of diverse edibles, planting kind of a "test garden."

It's so much fun to have a little extra space for trying something new, as you never know what you'll discover, like Siberian chives, which are kind of like regular chives but have a wonderful buttery onion flavor that can change up a salad. Plus, it looks beautiful in the garden. Or, perhaps, chocolate mint — it might sound like something that Willy Wonka would grow in his candy factory, but it's an actual plant. It smells similar to a peppermint patty and makes a fantastic tea that's great for soothing digestive ailments, just like traditional mint leaves.

When he traveled throughout the nation during its early years, and abroad, he often exchanged seeds and seedlings with other gardeners. He enjoyed cultivating those seeds and young plants in his Monticello garden. In fact, Jefferson once wrote, "The greatest service which can be rendered to any country is to add a useful plant to its culture."

His Designs

In Jefferson's extensive diary, which spans some 60 years starting from the age of 23, along with thousands of letters, he drew diagrams of his landscape and planting plans, keeping what were known as garden calendars. He laid out his garden in squares, with each square numbered. He spent time laying out the beds and planning just where his seeds would be planted. Because he grew a variety of crops, including a mix of both cool weather and tropical species, he came up with a unique terraced landscape for his vegetable garden. It was placed on a south-facing slope in order to capture the maximum amount of sunshine. This unique form of a "hanging garden" required some 600,000 cubic feet of red clay to be removed, and featured a tall, 1,000-foot-long rock wall.

I've tried all sorts of different gardening designs — it could really be called an art. It's a great way to discover new creative ways for growing more when you have limited space. These days there are so many options, from indoor container gardens to square foot gardening. But even if you have lots of space, there always seems to be a new and better way to organize it all.

I Grow What I Love to Eat

Jefferson loved to eat vegetables, so much that he once wrote that they constituted his principal diet. Exposed to such a wide range of different cuisine during his travels, he often brought recipes home for his cooks to get creative and use the garden produce in new ways. One of his recipes for okra soup includes ingredients from various continents; okra from the West Indies, lima beans from Native Americans, and tomatoes and potatoes from Europe.

Growing what I love to eat means I make the most out of what my garden produces while doing lots of tasty experimenting to come up with new, innovative ways to use the harvest in recipes.

Natural, Organic Gardening

Jefferson once told his daughter after she complained about insects devouring their garden vegetables, "I suspect that the insects which have harassed you have been encouraged by the feebleness of your plants; and that has been produced by the lean state of the soil."

As chemicals weren't an option back then, his recommendation was manure, advising that the garden be covered with a heavy coating during the winter in order to result in stronger, richer soil. And the result? Higher quality produce that was defiant to drought and pests.

That's just how I think of my gardening today: no pesticides used here when there are so many natural alternatives that served us far better back then, and today.

Detailed Records of Failure and Success

Jefferson was meticulous and had a scientist's mind, keeping detailed records of what worked and what didn't work in his garden. He carefully documented planting procedures, the spacings of rows, whenever blossoms appeared, and when plants were harvested. Hatch noted that he had a "zeal to categorize the world around him."

Jefferson wrote, "It is the failure of one thing that is repaired by the success of another."

It's interesting to read his notes as he was never afraid to admit when he failed. Some years, there would be a long list of failures but he simply continued on, keeping notes regardless of success or failure. He'd grow the crop that did well, and discard those that didn't meet his standards.

There are a couple of important lessons here, one being obvious, that failure is an important stepping stone to success. But the other lesson is that success is best accomplished by learning why failure happens. The only way to know the how's and why's is to keep detailed records.

Ten Reasons You Should Grow Your Own Food Today

While growing and preserving food is still a very common activity in many cultures around the world, it is not always so here in America. Many people take food for granted, simply going to the grocery store without much thought as to where the food comes from. We just expect it to be there, right?

I encourage you to imagine a world where grocery stores did not exist, where there would be no fresh veggies, fruit or herbs unless you grew them yourself. While you may think this could never happen, I urge you to consider the reality. We are living in fragile times — times that require us to prepare for the possibility of a severe food shortage.

Here are just some of the many reasons why you should consider growing at least some food in a home garden.

You Will Save Money

One of the factors that inspired me to start growing my own food was that it would save me money. Organic produce can be expensive… but a pack of organic seeds? Not so bad. With all things factored in, I can still save quite a bit of money when I grow my own plants over paying the high price at the grocery store.

For example, a bag of organic baby spinach costs around $4 at my local grocery store, and it's only enough for a few servings. Compare that to organic seeds which are a fraction of the cost, and will yield about six pounds of fresh spinach. To me, it makes great sense. And even if I do have to work a little for it, I can still enjoy fresh, organic spinach all season long.

You Will Be Healthier

Even more important than the savings is the opportunity to consume produce that is loaded with valuable nutrients. Food that's grown organically, without synthetic pesticides, contains more nutrients when compared to non-organic foods.

In an analysis of more than 300 studies published in 2014 in the _British Journal of Nutrition_, researchers found that organic crops, which included everything from blueberries and apples to broccoli and carrots, had a substantially higher concentration of antioxidants and other beneficial compounds. In just one example there were 50 percent more flavonols and anthocyanins in organic crops than conventional ones.

Plus, when you grow your own fruits and veggies, you tend to eat more of them. You also know more about what comes in contact with your food, and you can control when it's harvested. Store-bought produce is often harvested too early and is lacking in essential nutrients.

You Can Protect Your Kids

I remember reading some staggering statistics about how susceptible young children are to pesticides. That was over fifteen years ago, and things are worse today.

According to the National Academy of Sciences, children are much more susceptible to chemicals than adults. Estimates show that 50% of lifetime pesticide exposure occurs during the first five years of life. The average child receives four times more exposure than an adult to at least eight widely used cancer-causing pesticides in food.

If nothing else, this should encourage you to begin gardening for the health of your children.

You Will Be Prepared For a Food Shortage

During World War I, and especially World War II, Americans were asked to grow their own food to help support the war effort. Although we may not be in the middle of a world war, our food supply is extremely vulnerable nonetheless.

All you have to do is take a look around the world to see what might happen. In Venezuela, for example, citizens have been enduring a catastrophic food shortage, due to an economic crisis and total collapse of the food system that relied heavily on imported foods. As currency controls food imports, hyperinflation eats into salaries, and people line up for hours to buy basics like flour.

There are people starving in that country. And amid the crisis, the government advised Venezuelans to start growing their own food and raising their own chickens. But gardening takes time, and if you don't know anything about it, it can take even longer.

Regardless of the type of government or those who are in power, any population that relies on imports for its food supply could be next on the list to experience a dire food shortage. The United States imports more food than any other nation on the planet, followed by China, Germany, Japan and the United Kingdom.

There doesn't have to be a major economic crisis either. What happens if truck drivers go on strike or for some other reason the delivery trucks are unable to deliver food to the stores? What if there is a fuel shortage which prevents them from delivery, or causes the prices to skyrocket?

Taking action *now* is a must to prevent future tragedy.

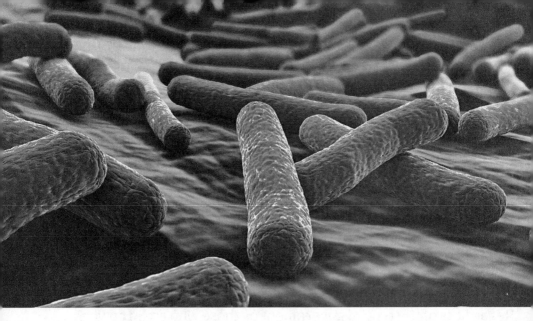

Safety

When you grow your own food, you know exactly where it came from. That way, the next time you read about some foodborne illness, you won't have to worry.

Remember the 2006 E. coli outbreak linked to spinach? Investigators were able to identify environmental risk factors, but they never could say just how the contamination originated. There was another E. coli outbreak linked to romaine lettuce earlier this year, which made nearly 60 people ill and killed at least two people. The list of other incidents is long. In fact, the FDA estimates that 48 million people become sick from a foodborne illness every year, and 3,000 die.

I don't know about you, but I like to know where my food comes from. And when I grow it myself, I can be assured my health and the health of my family is protected.

Your Food Will Be Fresh

Around <u>one-fifth of the fresh vegetables</u> in the United States come from overseas. How fresh can it be when it's had to travel thousands of miles? The quality of store-bought produce gets lower and lower the further it has to travel. So unless you're buying from the farm or a local farmer's market, you're probably not getting the freshest foods.

However, when you grow your own, it just doesn't get any fresher than that. You can choose when to harvest, and consume what you grow when it reaches peak ripeness. It naturally tastes much better this way. In fact, some have noted after growing their own food that they never really knew just how good a fresh tomato, ear of corn, or what have you, really was.

You'll Help the Planet

Our planet could really use some love, and when you grow your own food, you'll be benefiting the earth and our environment in a number of ways. First, you won't be polluting the air by driving to the grocery store.

Second, you'll be helping to cut back on the energy used by modern farming. Modern farming currently utilizes more petroleum than any other single industry! It consumes 12 percent of America's total energy supply. So if you grow your own, you're reducing pollution both from your travel and modern farm equipment.

You'll Get to Try New and Different Things

When you grow your own food you can have fun experimenting with all sorts of varieties. There are so many different types of seeds, you'll be able to choose from hundreds in all different colors, shapes and flavors.

Ever try a dragon fruit? Or how about Japanese wineberries, an ice cream banana or rainbow carrots? That's enough to get anyone excited about trying new fruits and vegetables, don't you think?

You Can Teach Your Kids

There are many great lessons you can teach your children, but one of the best is teaching them how to grow food and provide for themselves. Who knows what the world will be like when they grow up! Learning to be sustainable is one of the greatest tools you could ever give a child.

My children have always had their hands in the dirt, helping me in the garden from a very early age. They learned how to plant, care for and harvest food from the family garden. This skill was something that was very important to me as a parent to teach — much more important than teaching them how to follow a list at the grocery store.

You Will Be Less Stressed

There is nothing that reduces my blood pressure more than tending my garden. There is something incredibly relaxing about spending time caring for plants, watching them bend and reach for the sun, watching them produce delicious food for my table.

Science even confirms how valuable growing a garden can be to your mental health. One study asked volunteers to perform a stressful activity followed by either 30 minutes of reading indoors or 30 minutes of gardening. While both managed to reduce stress, gardening had a much more dramatic impact. All sorts of mental health experts and physicians have determined that getting out in the garden is great therapy. It's even being used to treat anxiety, depression, PTSD and Alzheimer's disease, among many other ailments.

Gardening also gets you moving, outside in the fresh air, requiring digging, planting, harvesting and so on, all of which is great low-impact exercise. Forty-five minutes of gardening burns about the same amount of calories as running a mile and a half in 15 minutes.

"My garden is my most beautiful masterpiece"

— Claude Monet

Why Monsanto is Not Welcome In My Garden — How to Keep GMOs Out

Unless you have been hiding under a rock, you have probably heard the name Monsanto. Monsanto is a company that specializes in poison and political manipulation, yet we're expected to put our trust in this organization that really doesn't have our best interests, or our planet's, in mind. Instead, it's all about the almighty dollar, with no cares or concerns about the current spike in chronic diseases like cancer, diabetes and obesity.

I often tell people, "Don't even get me started on Monsanto." I could talk all day about how horrible the company is for human and environmental health. Let me just share a few things.

ALTERNATIVE
DAILY

Roundup

I'm sure you've heard of the company's top-selling herbicide, Roundup, which is widely used across the country. Countless independent studies have linked the main ingredient in this product, glyphosate, to all sorts of health problems, including weaker immune systems, infertility, allergies and even cancer. It's also known to spread diseases in wheat, like Fusarium head blight, and has resulted in the spread of superweeds and increased use of chemicals in general.

The Devastating Effects of GMOs

The other problem I'm talking about is GMOs (genetically modified organisms) and the devastating effects of the Monsanto GMO monopoly on our food — our entire planet is groaning due to the abuse of corporate greed! Time is running out, with our own health and the health of the world depending on it. The biotech industry has been manipulating the genes of GMO sugar beets and alfalfa treated with Roundup. Many members of the scientific community have been warning of the dangers of GMO foods that can result in all sorts of serious health problems, including disease and organ failure. There is a growing stack of evidence that animals fed genetically modified crops have different immunological, physiological and metabolic responses compared to those who aren't fed GM crops.

Monsanto's GMO seeds are also devastating U.S. agriculture. The effects have been truly disastrous, with one recent report revealing GM crops have cost American taxpayers more than $12 billion in farm subsidies. The U.K. Soil Association reports that an investigation by the *New York Times* found that genetic modification hasn't delivered crop improvements like supporters of GM were promised. In fact, it's failed to increase crop yields, and it's also failed to reduce the overall use of pesticides on crops.

The Truth About GMOs

They don't live up to the hype. They don't do what they're supposed to do, with little to no yield improvements and just as many pesticides, if not more, required. Long-term studies of organic farming have found that organic can match the yields of conventional agriculture.

They increase corporate control over our food. The dozen or so brands you see in the supermarkets today are mostly owned by just a few parent companies. Whenever a company has a monopoly on a grocery store aisle or certain products, they make decisions based on their profits and not what's best for the planet — or their customers. Monsanto now owns an astounding number of seed companies that were once its competitors. What that means is that when a customer buys Monsanto seeds that were engineered to withstand Roundup, the gardener or farmer who plants these seeds often buys Roundup as well.

GMO foods and organic foods can't coexist. Trying to keep a farm or garden GMO-free can be difficult, as GMOs don't necessarily stay where they're planted. This means they often contaminate neighboring farms and gardens, sometimes even miles away due to the wind.

There is a lot of biased research. Although there has been a lot of research focused on the effects and safety of GMOs, much of it has been funded, conducted or influenced at least in part by the biotech industry. While the advocates claim there is a general consensus that scientists agree GMOs are safe, they have typically cherry-picked points from reports in order to cast them in a more positive light. Long-term, independent studies are what's truly needed in order to know the truth about GMOs, and their effects on the environment and our health.

The easiest option to ensure you're not eating genetically modified foods created by big biotech companies, like Monsanto, is to grow your own organic food.

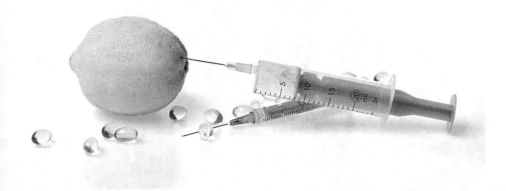

So How Can You Keep GMOs Out?

Seeds

It's that time of the year again, when seed companies fill mailboxes with catalogs offering all types of seeds for sowing in spring gardens. And one of the biggest concerns when it comes to keeping GMOs out of your garden is choosing the right seeds, which means only using seeds that are non-GMO and organic. But what many gardeners don't realize is that Monsanto has been gobbling up the seed market faster than that caterpillar can take down your tomato plant.

In 2005, the GMO titan grabbed up 40% of the vegetable seed market with its acquisition of Seminis. It also has the trademark for many of the names of the actual heirloom seed varieties too. That means that when you buy organic or heirloom seeds, even if it's from an independent company, some of that purchase may be going to support Monsanto.

When Purchasing Seeds:

Avoid purchasing from seed companies that are affiliated with Monsanto. There are still dozens of good seed companies that have signed the Safe Seed Pledge and tested their seeds to be free of GMOs. You can find a list published by the Council for Responsible Genetics at councilforresponsiblegenetics.org. It is incredibly important that we all support seed companies that are committed to the principles of preserving a safer and healthier food supply for future generations. If you're considering a seed company that isn't listed, don't hesitate to give them a call and ask what their policies are, and who they're owned by or affiliated with.

When Buying Starts:

When you purchase starts, be sure to buy only organic varieties and ask your local nursery or home garden store about GMOs. It's best to choose an organic nursery, and also talk to the staff about where their seeds come from. Do some research on high-risk plants too, and avoid them or be extra careful to choose non-GMO starts.

The Soil:

What your plants are grown in makes a big difference too, which means it's important to use organic compost and soil. You don't want to unknowingly plant in soil that was chemically contaminated. By choosing organic and speaking to the retail staff about where it comes from, you'll know exactly what kind of soil you're getting.

Keep in mind that good soil takes time. Prepare it bit by bit without expecting everything to be perfect all at once, as it can take years to create a very good garden. Keep adding organic matter to a compost pile, away from the growing area in order to allow insects to do what they do without interfering with what's growing in your garden. Then add the compost after a year of maturation. Remember that for everything you take from the soil you have to give back. Rotate plots and grow winter manure crops that can be plowed under in springtime in order to enrich the soil. Avoid growing the same intensity of veggies in the same plot every season. Follow a season of growing more demanding vegetables with one that's less demanding and so on.

When you're in the seasonal rhythm, you won't even need to use organic pesticides. When plants are grown in their season, they'll be able to stand up to disease, resist inclement weather and repel insects. If you plant a fall crop in the summer, it's going to need all of its energy just to survive, allowing pests or disease to easily take over.

Fertilizers, Additives and Natural Pest Fighting Alternatives

Be sure to talk to your local organic nursery to find help regarding additives that you may need, such as natural fertilizer. Local nursery staff typically serve as an excellent resource regarding the best varietals to select, your particular climate, handling pests and other issues. They can provide a wealth of information about gardening and how to keep GMOs out.

One Final Note

Remember that each step you take to speak and act out against GMOs, no matter how small, adds up when it comes to your health, the health of the community and the health of our planet.

 Don't forget: The corporate quest of Monsanto is to make money off each and every one of us, without any regard to our safety or the safety of future generations.

"Genetically modified (GM) foods may look and feel the same as conventional foods, but they are drastically (and possibly harmfully) different. These types of foods have been altered by taking the genetic material (DNA) from one species and transferring it into another in order to obtain a desired trait. The FDA does not require any safety testing or any labeling of GM foods, and introducing new genes into a fruit or vegetable may very well be creating unknown results such as new toxins, new bacteria, new allergens and new diseases."

— M.D. David Brownstein, The Guide to Healthy Eating

Are You Ready to Grow Organic?

Now is the time to embrace organic gardening. Here are some of the great things that I love about organic gardening and a few tips to get you started.

Fact: Some of the most commonly used chemicals for non-organic farming and gardening have been linked to cancer, autism, attention deficit disorders and many other chronic diseases. Avoiding synthetic chemical fertilizers, pesticides and fungicides means my garden is a safe place for birds to forage, bees to do their work and for children to play.

Love the Soil

Soil provides the nutrients that plants need to survive and thrive. With healthy, nutrient-rich soil, you'll get healthy, thriving plants. Drainage is another important factor because not many plants like wet feet. Waterlogging chokes the plant roots as the pores in the soil fill with water, and this promotes the growth of anaerobic bacteria that can cause root rot. The soil can also become too acidic due to the accumulation of carbon dioxide and other byproducts of bacterial decomposition.

Good quality garden compost, leaf mold, composted bark, well-rotted and aged manure are vital organic materials that should be incorporated into the soil. They increase aeration and drainage in fine, compacted clay-based soils. In addition to providing plenty of nutrients for plants, these materials absorb moisture like a sponge and retain it, so they are good for increasing water retention in fast-draining sandy soils too.

Make Your Own Compost

Although compost is readily available, you can avoid the recurring expense by making your own. It's also a great way to recycle almost all the organic waste generated in your house as well as the garden, and composting garden and kitchen waste onsite reduces the burden on landfills. If you need a lot of compost, you can source free organic materials such as lawn trimmings, leaf litter, coffee grounds and wood chips easily retained from local businesses. Many times, they are more than willing to supply what you need.

A compost pit in a corner of the garden or an open or closed compost bin is easy to manage. Just be sure to use the correct ratio of green materials and brown materials for best results. An ideal compost pile should start with a 30:1 C/N ratio. Fresh grass clippings alone have about a 20:1 C/N ratio. Building your pile with one part grass clippings or other green matter to two parts dead leaves or other brown matter will give you the right mix. If you don't want the hassle of turning compost and then lugging the finished product to garden beds, you can try trench composting where you dump all the waste in trenches, cover it with soil and then plant over it the next season.

Select Disease-Resistant Varieties of Plants

Organic gardening is all about avoiding chemicals of all types. However, some plant diseases are devastating, quickly spreading through an entire crop and destroying it. Diseases may be caused by bacteria, fungi or viruses. Viral diseases do not have any remedies, but when bacterial and fungal diseases affect the plants, chemical fungicides and bactericides often provide quick results. Although it is tempting to use these chemical-based solutions, it's important to avoid them as they enter our produce directly through plant tissue or by way of contaminated air and water.

Getting disease-resistant varieties is the best bet for organic gardens. Plant breeders have developed many cultivars that are highly resistant to viral diseases, bacterial rot and fungal infections, and not all of them are GMO plants as many gardeners fear. Selective breeding and hybridization with naturally resistant wild varieties have produced many strains with reliable disease resistance. Another option is to look for heirloom varieties that have developed high levels of disease resistance.

Grow More Local Varieties

Seeds and starts you need for the garden are best sourced locally from established nurseries or farms. Mail order catalogs may offer many high-yielding varieties and newly developed hybrids, but you have no way of knowing whether they are suitable for your climate and soil conditions. The USDA zones are just a general guide for selecting plant varieties, basically telling you whether a plant is hardy enough to survive in the temperature range normally experienced in your area. It does not take into consideration the wind, precipitation, heat and humidity that determine the microclimate of a given place.

Local varieties are acclimatized to the climate and seasonal variations. They are more likely to be resistant to pests and diseases. Pollinators in the locality usually gravitate towards familiar varieties of plants. Try to find the high yielding and disease-resistant varieties popular in your specific locality by consulting other gardening enthusiasts that live close to you.

Get Organic Mulch or Make Your Own

Mulches, by definition, are materials used to cover the soil's surface to lock in moisture and to suppress weeds. They also reduce diseases by acting as a barrier between the crops and the soil containing many pathogens. They can be organic, such as wood chips, straw and pine needles. Natural inorganic materials like pea gravel, river stones and lava rock make long-lasting mulches, as do black plastic sheet mulch and shredded rubber mulch, but they don't do much in the way of enriching the soil.

Any type of mulch, even plastic mulch, may be better than no mulch, but organic types of mulch are the best choice for organic gardening because they gradually break down, increasing the humus content and nutrient levels as well as nurturing many beneficial organisms in the soil. Use lots of crushed leaves and grass clippings as mulch around your plants and around walkways.

ALTERNATIVE DAILY

Raise Chickens and Other Farm Animals

The benefits of having a few chickens in an organic garden are many. Apart from providing healthy, organic eggs, they act as instant composters, eating up almost any edible thing, be it vegetable peels, leftover food or garden waste. They are excellent at pest control too, devouring grasshoppers, caterpillars and insects hiding under leaves. Their constant scratching exposes many larvae that live among the soil and mulch. But the best part of all is that they can provide you with high-quality manure.

Raising turkeys, sheep, goats and/or rabbits are also great choices for organic gardens that can accommodate them. Turkey manure is nitrogen rich, while sheep manure contains a high potash content. Manure of herbivorous animals is safer added to the soil without any treatment, especially rabbit droppings as it breaks down quickly without burning plant roots.

Harvest and Store Rainwater

Water, along with sunlight, is the lifeforce of any garden. I have been harvesting rain from my roof for many years. No matter where you live, it is a good thing to install a rain harvesting system. This could be something as simple as a few rain barrels or as complex as underground water storage system. Either way, harvesting the rain that comes off of your roof is just another way to ensure your sustainability.

Rainwater is ideal for plants because of its slightly acidic nature that most vegetables prefer. Most municipal water supplies, on the other hand, tend to be slightly alkaline, artificially made in order to protect plumbing lines. Well water in most places is hard due to salts and other minerals in the soil and rocks that leach into the water.

Consider Moving Water

There is nothing I like more than moving water in my garden. Water attracts all kinds of pollinators and also acts as a natural humidifier. Not to mention the fact that water adds a beautiful and relaxing element to any outdoor space.

As soon as a pond is established, a unique ecosystem develops around it. You can grow many edible plants and herbs such as watercress, taro, water chestnut, pennyroyal and water mint in and around the pond. It can house a number of fish too, both edible and ornamental, but more importantly, it sustains a variety of wildlife such as frogs and dragonflies. Water attracts birds and bats too, which are very good at pest control.

If you have fish in the pond, the water is enriched with nutrients that can be used to water the plants. Mosquitoes are rarely a problem in such ponds since fish and frogs usually take care of them as part of their diet.

Throw Flowering Plants and Herbs into the Mix

Wind accidentally pollinates the flowers of many vegetables and fruit trees, but insect pollinators do the best job when they visit flowers. That's why tomato flowers visited by bumblebees produce larger tomatoes. Grow flowering plants and herbs among your vegetables to attract bees. Many pollinators are plant-specific, meaning they only visit certain plants. For instance, squash bees gather pollen exclusively from the flowers of cucurbit family plants. Legumes are mostly pollinated by bumblebees and fruit trees by mason bees.

Most of the pollinating insects have a limited territory from where they collect pollen and nectar, so it makes sense to attract them into the garden by offering suitable habitats for them.

Organic gardens free of chemicals do offer a safe foraging field for these beneficial insects, but they should ideally take up residence there. Leave some remote corners of the garden undisturbed to allow ground nesters like squash bees, mining bees and sweat bees to nest in your garden.

Biological Pest Control with Plants and Predatory Bugs

Even if you grow an all-organic garden, you will still have to deal with pests. Garden pests have many natural enemies that can act as biological control agents, including predators like carnivorous insects as well as parasites and disease-causing microbes.

Luring predators like praying mantises, ladybugs, hoverflies and lacewings into your garden is one way to control pest populations. Many nectar-producing flowers attract these insects. Grow yarrow, mint, lavender, dill and parsley among the vegetables. When these beneficial insects breed in the garden, their voracious larvae are even more predatory.

Sometimes predatory insects may have to be introduced into the garden. Predator eggs and adults can be purchased online or from bug farms. Commercial products containing fungal spores that infect insects are also available and are effective against a wide range of pests like aphids, whiteflies, Colorado potato beetle, caterpillars, grasshoppers and mealy bugs.

Be Creative

I love the fact that there are so many time-tested ways to organic garden. Hugelkultur and keyhole garden are two techniques that allow you to grow vegetables on and around composted materials. A little bit of soil and all types of debris heaped over rotting logs and twigs form the basis of hugelkultur. A keyhole garden is a circular raised bed constructed around a central compost heap. Nutrients are gradually released from the organic matter into the surrounding soil. I have had great success with this type of garden, especially in arid climates.

Straw bale gardening is another promising method that can help you overcome problem soils and uncultivable land. Plants are grown in pockets of compost in bales of pre-conditioned straw. As the plants grow and send out roots into the straw bale, it decomposes to provide the nutrients they need. This is a one-stop solution for rocky terrain, extremely clayey or acidic soils and nematode-infested areas. If you're going to use straw bales, be sure to wet them several days in a row before you plant. This will help encourage decomposition.

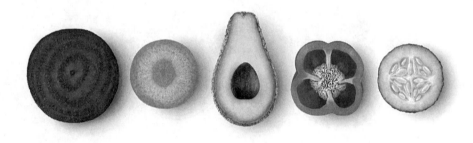

"The first supermarket supposedly appeared on the American landscape in 1946. That is not very long ago. Until then, where was all the food? Dear folks, the food was in homes, gardens, local fields and forests. It was near kitchens, near tables, near bedsides. It was in the pantry, the cellar, the backyard."

— Joel Salatin

Vegetable Growing Tips

When it comes to growing vegetables, there are a number of important factors to consider, from selecting the type of plants and garden location to the best gardening methods, watering and everything in between.

Here are some great tips to get you started on your journey to sustainability:

Selecting the Crops

The vegetables you frequently buy and your family likes to eat are the obvious first choice for your vegetable garden. Tomatoes, potatoes, cucumbers, peppers, beans, radishes, spinach, and lettuce are garden staples, but try to include a row or two of specialty crops to experiment with. Some of my favorite include celeriac, white beets, bulb fennel, radicchio, escarole and Asian greens.

You should also consider dedicating a corner of the vegetable garden to crops that come back year after year. There's nothing like picking the freshest asparagus spears and rhubarb from your own garden in spring while other crops are still starting out.

Regardless of the vegetables you and your family prefer, one of the most important criteria for selecting crops to grow in your garden is which varieties do best in your area. Local farmers, nurseries and garden centers can provide invaluable tips to help you make the best choices. Choosing disease-resistant cultivars whenever possible is another important factor in order to avoid the need for chemical sprays in your vegetable patch.

Location

Carefully choose where your vegetable garden will be located. Most vegetables need full sun to do their best, ideally at least eight hours of sun each day. Root vegetables can do with five to six hours in the sun, with the rest in partial shade, and a few leafy vegetables can manage in filtered light. But fruiting vegetables do poorly if the sunlight is insufficient.

Avoid areas that fall under the shade of large trees or buildings. If the garden has to be set against the house, west and southwest sides are better choices. Proximity to the house is also important. Locate the garden where you can easily give your crops the attention they require to do their best.

Lay of the land is another consideration; choose level ground or slightly elevated areas that gently slope away to facilitate natural drainage during rain. Keep in mind that waterlogging can make the soil too acidic.

Seeds Vs. Starts

I generally use a combination of seeds and starts in my garden. It is important to note that you may not always get the expected results with seeds collected from standing crops or from the produce you buy at the supermarket. Most of these are hybrids which display desirable characteristics only for a single generation and then revert to the original traits of their parents in subsequent generations.

Open pollinated heirloom varieties are an exception; they almost always live up to expectation and typically have better disease resistance as well. Local farmers are the best sources for heirloom seeds of the varieties that do well in your area. You can also buy the seeds of named hybrid varieties from reputed suppliers.

If you have a short growing season, you need to start your seeds indoors six to eight weeks early and then harden them up gradually before planting outside in spring.

Buying nursery starts can be expensive, but they are more reliable and can be planted directly into the garden. They may even work out to be cost effective if you can buy in bulk.

Where Does Your Garden Grow?

One of my favorite ways to make a healthy garden bed is to double dig and turn over compost and other soil amendments. This raises the beds a few inches from the ground, facilitating good drainage and better root run. In areas with heavy rain, water-logging can be avoided by digging trenches between the beds and piling the extra soil on the beds, raising it further.

The shape and size of the beds matter too. Long beds that are more than four feet wide are not practical. When they're too long it makes gardening chores like tending to the plants, weeding and harvesting difficult. Circular beds can be five feet wide since they provide good access from all around; building them in an arched shape can increase the soil surface available for planting.

If you don't have the time and patience to cultivate the land, build raised beds above the ground with wooden boards, cinder blocks, sandbags or other recycled materials. Fill them with good soil and compost, and then plant immediately. I love to garden using raised beds when I am short on space.

Container Growing

Container gardening is ideal for small spaces and in areas where there is a short growing season. You can start the crop early in a sheltered area and then move the pots to more exposed locations. Place the pots on a wheeled platform to make shifting easier.

You have a choice of using plastic, clay, metal or wooden containers for growing vegetables. The need to water the plants more frequently is a problem with container gardens because the soil dries out faster and the plant roots cannot go anywhere else looking for moisture.

Using larger containers and mass planting can reduce water loss to some extent, though more frequent feeding may be necessary. It is best to discard growing media in the container after every crop since the plants will have exhausted all the nutrients.

Intensive Gardening Methods

Getting maximum yield from minimum space is the main intention of intensive methods of vegetable gardening, but they are not just for small gardens. By concentrating your efforts on a smaller area, you can save time and money as well, since soil preparation, soil amendments, watering, feeding and weeding are minimized.

Raised Beds

As mentioned, raised beds are a one-stop solution for poor soil and uneven or rocky terrain. Close planting of different types of vegetables optimizes space, chokes out weeds and reduces moisture loss from soil surface. Straw bale gardening, mentioned earlier, is another great way to grow a number of plants in a relatively small space.

Interplanting and Crop Succession

Interplanting and crop successions means growing two or more compatible crops in the same bed at the same time. For example, interplant broccoli or beans with radishes or lettuce. Mixing long-season crops with short-season ones and starting successive crops as soon one is harvested also puts the vegetable patches to maximum use.

Vertical Growing

You can reduce competition for space by training sprawling plants up a supporting structure. Pole beans, peas, melons, cucumbers and tomatoes can be supported by poles, trellises or strings attached to vertical frames, freeing up the ground for leafy vegetables and root crops that can tolerate some amount of shade.

Watering

Vegetable gardens require timely watering, especially in the warmer months. Rapid water loss through the leaves can cause wilting, which can adversely affect the health of the plants and reduce yield too. Water stress and frequent wilting cycles will also make the crops more susceptible to diseases.

A soaker hose running along the length of your garden beds can keep them well hydrated. The frequency of watering should also be adjusted depending on the humidity, temperature, wind and other atmospheric conditions prevailing at the time.

Deep watering at longer intervals is generally preferable to frequent shallow watering. You may also want to give an occasional soaking to the entire crop with a hand-held hose in order to clean the leaves of dust and dislodge pests.

Setting up a drip irrigation system with a timer can make it easy to automate watering, something that's helpful whether you're at home or away on vacation. It conserves water, providing it close to the root ball of each plant. Another advantage of drip irrigation is that it reduces weed growth. If you have a rainwater harvesting system, it can be connected to the irrigation line.

Don't Forget to Feed Your Plants

Amending the soil with good quality compost and well-rotted manure can provide all the nutrients plants need, but occasional supplemental feeding with mineral fertilizers is a good idea for giving them a boost.

Plants need nitrogen, phosphorus and potassium in large amounts and several trace elements in small quantities. Commercial NPK fertilizers contain these substances in the right proportions, so using them at regular intervals can prevent nutrient deficiencies. But of course for growing vegetables organically, you'll need to consider natural alternatives to chemical fertilizers.

Add some unflavored gelatin granules to the soil when you sow seeds or transplant seedlings, which provides nitrogen when plants most need it. This element helps to instill good foliage growth. Blood meal and rock phosphate are good natural sources of phosphorus, while kelp meal, greensand and hardwood ashes are rich in potassium.

Companion Planting

Planting certain crops close to one another is beneficial. While one provides support or shade for the companions, another may help keep weeds or pests down. You may be familiar with the "three sisters" combination that Native Americans popularized. This consists of corn, pole beans and pumpkins, with the growing corn providing light shade to the young bean seedlings which will eventually climb on the cornstalk. The pumpkin will spread all over the ground, keeping it weed-free and insulated.

Some plants like marigolds, garlic, chives and nasturtiums are welcomed as companion plants in vegetable gardens for their capacity to protect the crops from pests, either by repelling them or by attracting prospective pests to themselves. A few others, like basil and borage, are said to improve the flavor of their companions.

Just as there are plants that enjoy each others' company, there are others that would rather not share a row — or a garden bed for that matter. Beans and onion family plants don't go together; broccoli and Brussels sprouts should not be planted near your strawberry patch. Rue and fennel have to be kept away from your vegetable beds. If you aren't sure, talk to a knowledgeable person at your local nursery. Please refer to the "friends" and "enemies" sections of the veggie and content for companion planting information.

Beat Pesky Pests at Their Own Game

Before starting a veggie garden in your area, do some research to identify the most aggressive pests that may find your garden tasty. Once you have done this, it is wise to develop a defense strategy.

One of my favorite ways to naturally keep pests at bay is to use what I call combat plants — plants that naturally help with pest control. Marigolds are my favorite happy little flower to plant in and around my veggie garden. A significant number of pests find these beauties repulsive. Borage repels tomato worms and radishes repel cucumber beetles. Onions, garlic, chives and leeks planted in a carrot patch will keep carrot flies away. Several strong-smelling plants like catmint, lemongrass and thyme also act as insect repellents and can be planted all over your garden. Some plants protect crops by providing an alternative source of food for pests. For example, nasturtiums attract aphids to themselves and act as a host plant for cabbage moth eggs and larvae.

I also use diatomaceous earth, which occurs naturally in lake beds. It is actually made up of the fossils of single-celled planktonic algae that lived in lakes and oceans a very long time ago. Diatomite is rich in silica and has an abrasive, chalk-like texture.

Food grade diatomaceous earth is a non-toxic way to repel pests in the garden. It works for any pests that crawl because the powder is dehydrating. After you water your plants, dust them with the powder for protection. Do not apply to flowers.

Another trick I have learned through the years is to use a little bit of Castile soap mixed with water as a pest spray. I add one teaspoon of soap to a spray bottle and fill with water. The fatty acids in the soap break down the outer shell of many pests. To really go gangster on pests, add one teaspoon of hot sauce to the mixture and spray whenever you see pests.

Harvesting

The key to a successful garden is to encourage plants to continue to produce throughout the season. To do this, it is best to harvest for the table as soon as they are ready. This promotes continued production, especially in the case of cucumbers and tomatoes. For leafy vegetables, like lettuce and spinach, either the outer leaves can be picked regularly or the whole plant can be harvested when it reaches a good size.

Large-scale harvesting is done when you want to sell the produce or preserve them by pickling or canning. Vegetables harvested when they are tender taste better and remain crisp when refrigerated, but mature melons and gourds, onions and garlic can keep well for months without refrigeration.

Sun drying, salting and pickling in vinegar are low-key ways to preserve vegetables, but a deep freezer, food dehydrator and canning equipment are good investments when you grow a lot of vegetables.

If you have heirloom varieties, allow some fruit to mature and ripen on the plant to collect seeds for the next season.

"Odd as I am sure it will appear to some, I can think of no better form of personal involvement in the cure of the environment than that of gardening. A person who is growing a garden, if he is growing it organically, is improving a piece of the world. He is producing something to eat, which makes him somewhat independent of the grocery business, but he is also enlarging, for himself, the meaning of food and the pleasure of eating."

— Wendell Berry

Let's Get Growing — Vegetables

It's time to get our hands dirty. Here are my favorite veggies to grow and all the information you need to get started. Have fun.

ASPARAGUS

Though this plant can take a few years to truly become productive, it yields a bountiful harvest once established. This sun-loving perennial is one of the first crops that will be ready to eat each spring. Boil or steam this delicious vegetable and drizzle with a light vinaigrette for a healthy snack.

Popular Varieties:

- Purple passion
- "Jersey" series
- White asparagus

Soil:

- Allow plenty of room for drainage, as standing water is detrimental to plant health
- Cultivate rich, fertilized soil with manure and compost

Planting:

- Start from 1-year-old plants for easier cultivation
- Plant in early spring as soon as ground thaws
- Plant in 6-inch deep trenches
- Top with 2 to 3 inches of soil

Light:

- Grow in full sun

Growing:

- Top with soil periodically to allow for settling
- Form soil mounds around plants, leaving 2 to 3 feet exposed
- Weed often to prevent overcrowding
- Water regularly, but do not soak

- Aphid
- Asparagus beetle
- Asparagus rust
- Crown rot
- Slugs
- Gopher

Harvesting:

- Do not harvest in the first season, as asparagus needs time to get established
- Let plants go to foliage in the first year and cut them to ground level when they turn brown
- In the second season, harvest over a 4-week period
- By the third year, extend harvest season to 8 to 10 weeks
- Cut or snip off asparagus stalks at the base at an angle

Storage:

- Freeze any excess in airtight bags

Friends:

- Basil
- Parsley
- Tomato

Enemies:

- Garlic
- Onion
- Potato

 Did you know? Asparagus was Thomas Jefferson's favorite vegetable.

BEETS

Beets can be cooked in a variety of ways and pack a nutritional punch. Though the bulbous parts of beets are most commonly served, the greens are delicious and contain even more iron than spinach. This annual plant must be sown every year, but is incredibly easy to start from seed and one of the hardiest crops to grow.

Popular Varieties:

- Yellow
- White
- Detroit dark red
- Cylindra
- Semiglobe
- Globe

Soil:

- Ensure that your soil is deep enough, as beets can grow as long as 8 inches
- Allow for good drainage
- Clear all rocks from growing area
- Cultivate loose, light soil with compost and manure

Planting:

- Start from seed in mid-spring to early summer
- Plant seeds 1-inch deep and 1-inch apart
- Cover with a light layer of soil and gently pat down

Light:

- Grow in full sun

Growing:

- Water at least 1 inch per week to prevent bolting and flowering
- Thin out seedlings to 4 inches apart
- Weed carefully in the early stages, making sure not to disturb delicate sprouts

Threats:

- Leaf miner
- Flea beetle

Harvesting:

- Pull or dig out beets in late spring when roots reach 1 inch in diameter
- Do not allow beets to grow larger than 3 inches, as the flavor will diminish and they will become bitter

Storage:

- Beet greens and roots can be frozen in an airtight bags
- Store roots for up to 6 months by layering roots between sand, peat or sawdust in sealed boxes

Friends:

- Head lettuce
- Garlic
- Onion

Enemies:

- Pole bean

 Did you know? The largest beet ever recorded was grown by a Dutchman and weighed over 156 pounds!

BROCCOLI

Though slightly more difficult to grow than other vegetables, the payoff is well worth it. This hearty green crop is rich in vitamins and minerals and delicious when steamed or eaten raw. With a little bit of care and attention, this annual plant will flourish.

Popular Varieties:

- Green goliath
- Calabrese
- Chinese broccoli
- Di Cicco
- Packman
- Marathon

Soil:

- Slightly acidic soil allows for best growth
- Cultivate fertile soil with compost or manure

Planting:

- Plant early in the spring or fall season, as seeds can germinate in soil temperatures as low as 40 degrees Fahrenheit
- Broccoli thrives in cooler weather so do not plant if the days are getting hot
- Plant in rows, 1/2-inch deep and 12 inches apart

Light:

- Grow in full sun, but if the temperature begins to warm, provide partial shade with a shade cloth or awning

Growing:

- Thin seedlings to 12 inches apart
- Keep soil moist with regular watering, but ensure appropriate drainage to prevent waterlogging seedlings (1 to 1 1/2 inches per week)
- Focus water at the roots to avoid wetting heads
- Fertilize with a compost tea or blood meal
- Suffocate weeds with mulch rather than weed-pulling as broccoli roots are delicate
- When daytime temperatures exceed 75 degrees Fahrenheit, lay down a thick layer of mulch to contain moisture and cool plants

Threats:

- Aphid
- Cabbage butterfly
- Black rot
- Flea beetle
- Downy mildew
- Cabbage looper
- Clubroot
- Whitefly

Harvesting:

- Harvest before the heads flower and before yellow petals start to appear
- Cut heads from plant, just below where the stems begin to separate, leaving at least 6-inches of stem
- Side-shoots will keep developing after you harvest the main head and as long as the weather remains sufficient

Storage:

- Pickle broccoli in jars
- Refrigerate for up to 1 week in vegetable crisper
- Freeze in airtight container

Friends:

- Artichoke
- Beet
- Bush bean
- Cucumber
- Lettuce
- Potato
- Spinach

Enemies:

- Snap bean
- Strawberry
- Tomato

Did you know? Romans were eating this vegetable as early as 6,000 BCE in the Mediterranean.

BRUSSELS SPROUTS

These mini cabbage-like vegetables, when cooked properly, are delicious and nutrient-rich. Brussels sprouts are late to mature and prefer colder weather over hot summer temperatures. As with other members of the brassica family, these sprouts are susceptible to pests and diseases.

Popular Varieties:

- Jade cross
- Long Island improved

Soil:

- Raised beds are recommended in order to more effectively regulate soil and protect from inconsistent temperature

Planting:

- Start Brussels sprouts from seed or seedling about 4 months before first fall frost
- Light overnight frosts will help bring out sweet flavor, so time the planting accordingly
- Plant seeds 1/2-inch deep and 2 to 3 inches apart

Light:

- Grow in spots that allow for at least 6 hours of full sun per day

Growing:

- As the sprouts grow, they may require staking for extra support since their roots are not deep
- Remove yellow leaves to allow room for new growth
- When 6 inches tall, thin plants to 12 inches apart
- Provide at least 1 inch of water per week, careful not to overwater
- Hand-pull the weeds
- Mulch lightly to retain moisture

Threats:

- Blackleg
- Black rot
- Aphid
- Cabbage butterfly
- Cabbage root maggot
- Clubroot

Harvesting:

- Only harvest when temperature is near freezing
- Harvest from the bottom of the stalk up, gradually reaping bulbs
- When sprouts are 1 inch in diameter and firm, twist them from the stem to break them off
- Pinch the top of stalks to direct nutrients towards the bottom of the stalk

Storage:

- Do not wash sprouts before storage, only before eating
- Store in plastic bag in refrigerator for up to 2 weeks
- Freeze Brussels sprouts for later use

Friends:

- Artichoke
- Beet
- Peas
- Potato
- Spinach

Enemies:

- Pole bean
- Strawberry
- Tomato

Did you know? If your Brussels sprouts smell like sulfur, you have most likely overcooked them.

CABBAGE

With a little effort, your cabbage crop can stay healthy and produce a bountiful harvest. This annual comes in many varieties from green to red and late season to early season. Do some research to find out which cabbage variety best suits your garden needs.

Popular Varieties:

- Primax
- Gonzales
- Chinese cabbage
- Golden acre

Soil:

- Early season cabbages do best in light, loamy soil, while late season varieties flourish with a heavier soil
- Cultivate soil with rich compost as cabbage is a heavy feeder

Planting:

- Plant seeds 4 weeks before last expected frost date in indoor containers, keeping soil moist
- Space seeds 2 inches apart and a 1/4-inch deep
- Transplant outdoors when seedlings have 3 leaves
- In outdoor garden, grow seedlings in rows 6 to 12 inches apart
- The closer together you plant cabbage, the smaller and sweeter the heads will be

Light:

- Grow in full sun for early crop
- For later season crop planted in midsummer, allow for afternoon shade

Growing:

- Provide thick mulch cover to retain moisture
- Hand-pull weeds to prevent damage to fragile cabbage roots
- Water regularly when plant is young but try not to wet the heads or leaves as this can lead to disease
- Mature plants need at least 2 inches of water per week

Threats:

- Blackleg
- Black rot
- Aphid
- Cabbage butterfly
- Cabbage root maggot
- Clubroot
- Splitting

Harvesting:

- Cabbage usually reaches full maturity in 70 days
- When heads are firm, cut off with a sharp knife
- Leave roots and leaves for a residual harvest of mini cabbage heads

Storage:

- Keep heads in damp, cool root cellar for up to 3 months
- Store in refrigerator, wrapped loosely in plastic for up to 2 weeks

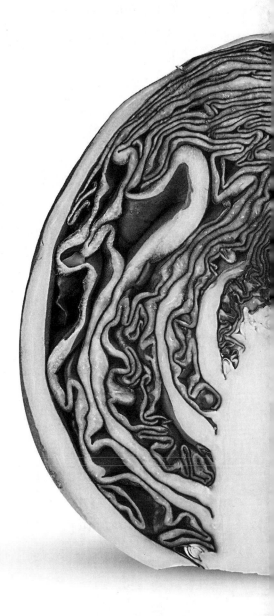

Friends:

- Beans
- Cucumber
- Artichoke
- Beet
- Lettuce
- Spinach

Enemies:

- Strawberry
- Tomato
- Broccoli
- Cauliflower
- Basil

 Did you know? Red cabbage can be utilized as a potent dye for food or fabric.

CARROTS

These crunchy roots are a favorite selection for salads and can be prepared in a variety of ways to utilize their sweet flavor. Though orange is the most common color for carrots, they grow in many different shades such as purple, red, yellow and even white. Carrots are an annual, cool-season crop that can be planted in the fall in warmer regions but are generally a spring vegetable.

Popular Varieties:

- Chantenay
- Danvers
- Imperator
- Nantes

Soil:

- Clear all stones from planting area to prevent misshapen carrots
- Cultivate deep, loose soil
- Avoid excessive amounts of fertilizer or manure

Planting:

- Start carrots from seed in early spring, 2 weeks before last expected frost
- Plant in rows, 6 seeds for every inch of soil
- Cover with a light layer of soil and gently water
- Allow 1 to 3 weeks to sprout
- Keep soil moist but not flooded

Light:

- Grow in full sun

Growing:

- Keep roots covered with a light layer of mulch to protect carrots from sun and retain moisture
- Thin when seedlings are 2 inches high so that plants are 1 inch apart
- Thin again 2 weeks later so that plants are 3 to 4 inches apart
- Water at least 1 inch per week
- Weed as often as needed to ensure carrots have enough room to grow

Threats:

- Deer
- Gopher
- Rabbit
- Woodchuck
- Rust fly
- Leaf blight
- Aster yellows disease
- Wireworm

Harvesting:

- Carrots generally take 2 to 4 months to reach full maturity
- Hand-pull carrots to prevent bruised roots

Storage:

- Twist off tops and wash off excess dirt
- Transfer to an airtight bag, dry and refrigerate until ready to eat
- Carrots can be left in the ground for as long as desired before the weather becomes hot.
- Keep tops covered with a loose layer of mulch or shredded leaves

Friends:

- Tomato
- Leek
- Beans

Enemies:

- Coriander
- Dill
- Parsnip

Did you know? Carrots are rich in beta-carotene, which converts to vitamin A and can help improve eyesight.

CORN

There are few foods that more vividly conjure up images of summer BBQs, picnics and Fourth of July celebrations than classic sweet corn. This delectable veggie is best enjoyed covered in butter and salt and paired with a refreshing watermelon. Though this crop takes up a lot of space, if you have the room, the results are well worth it.

Popular Varieties:

- Lochief
- Silver Queen
- Pristine
- Challenger Crisp 'N Sweet

Soil:

- Corn needs rich soil to flourish. For best results, till compost and manure into plot the fall before
- Soil should be 60 degrees Fahrenheit or warmer. Cover with black plastic and plant seeds through holes if necessary

Planting:

- Wait 2 weeks after last spring frost to plant from seed
- Plant in blocks, 3 rows wide
- Sow 3 seeds together in 1-inch deep holes every 7 to 15 inches
- Water well right after planting

Light:

- Grow in full sun

Growing:

- Thin to 1 plant every 15 inches of growth
- Weed frequently, careful not to damage roots
- Keep corn well-watered, layer with mulch if necessary to retain moisture and prevent weeds

Threats:

- Aphid
- Birds
- Corn borer
- Corn earworm
- Bacterial wilt
- Cutworm
- Flea beetle
- Cucumber beetle

Harvesting:

- About 3 weeks after corn silks appear, pull down husks to check for ripeness
- When milky liquid comes out of kernels when pierced, corn is ready for harvest
- Pull ears downward and twist to remove from stalk

Storage:

- Eat corn immediately if possible
- Sweet corn freezes well in airtight container

Friends:

- Cucumber
- Melon
- Pumpkin
- Squash
- Beans

Enemies:

- Tomato

 Did you know? Corn is a human invention and would not exist without cultivation.

CUCUMBERS

This crisp, green crop is not only delicious when sprinkled with salt and vinegar fresh off the vine, but is also delectable when pickled. Make a refreshing face mask by blending cucumber and applying in a thin layer to clean skin. This hardy annual flourishes in hot conditions and full sun.

Popular Varieties:

- Burpless bush hybrid
- Boston pickling
- Calypso

Soil:

- Cucumbers love light clay soil with humus
- Cultivate nutrient-rich soil with compost and manure
- Ensure proper drainage

Planting:

- Wait at least 1 week after the last frost to plant seeds when soil is 70 degrees Fahrenheit or warmer
- Cover planting area with black plastic and plant seeds through holes if necessary
- Plant in hills 3 to 5 inches apart with 6 to 8 seeds per hill
- Alternatively, plant in rows, sowing seeds 1-inch deep and 4 inches apart

Light:

- Grow in full sun

Growing:

- Mulch with pine straw or chopped leaves to keep pests away and hold in moisture
- Thin to the 3 best seedlings per hill once they are 2 inches tall. Cut unwanted seedlings away rather than pulling them up
- If planting in rows, thin seedlings to 1 inch apart
- Consider training cucumbers to climb trellises to keep crop off the ground and save space
- Always water at base of plant to prevent mold
- Keep soil moist and water often. Or consider setting up a soaker hose or irrigation system
- Spray vines with sugar water mixture to attract bees and increase pollination

Threats:

- Aphid
- Cucumber beetle
- Cutworm
- Squash bug
- Powdery mildew

Harvesting:

- Regular slicing cucumber varieties should be harvested when they are 6 to 8 inches long
- Do not wait too long to harvest or the crop will become bitter
- Cut the stem above the cucumber with a knife or scissors. Do not twist or pull
- Ensure that you are are checking for ripe cucumbers daily. They will mature quickly during harvest season

Storage:

- Wrap tightly in plastic to preserve freshness
- Store in refrigerator for up to 10 days in plastic
- Pickle for delicious, long-term storage

Enemies:

- Basil
- Potato
- Rosemary
- Sage

Friends:

- Beans
- Cabbage
- Eggplant
- Melon
- Peas
- Sunflower
- Tomato

 Did you know? Pressing a slice of cucumber to the roof of your mouth for 30 seconds can help eliminate bad breath.

EGGPLANT

These crops will mature in the peak of grilling season, making the perfect addition to any backyard party. Experiment with different types of eggplant, from lavender to snowy white, adding color and delicious flavor to every garden harvest.

Popular Varieties:

- Black beauty
- Little fingers
- Easter egg
- Ichiban
- Snowy
- Fairytale

Soil:

- Try growing eggplant in raised beds which heat up quickly in spring
- Mix 1 inch well-rotted manure into prepared bed

Planting:

- Start eggplants indoors 6 to 9 weeks before the last expected frost date
- Soak seeds overnight to encourage germination
- Sow seeds 1/4-inch deep in a loose, fine soil such as vermiculite
- Transplant seedlings to individual pots once they reach 3 inches
- Gradually expose them to outdoor temperatures to harden them off
- Once outdoor air warms up to 70 degrees Fahrenheit, transplant outdoors
- Space plants 2 1/2 to 3 inches apart in all directions
- Water well and pat soil down firmly

Light:

- Grow in full sun

Growing:

- Mulch immediately after transplanting
- Add stakes to the garden to provide support for plants
- Hand-pull any invading weeds, making sure not to disrupt roots
- Water 1 1/2 to 2 inches per week. Use a drip irrigation system or soaker hose to provide consistent watering

Threats:

- Flea beetle
- Tomato hornworm
- Verticillium wilt

Harvesting:

- Harvest eggplant 16 to 18 weeks after sowing when skin is shiny and unwrinkled
- Cut off eggplant from stem with sharp knife, leaving 1 inch of stem attached

Storage:

- Eggplant can be stored for up to 2 weeks in warm, humid environment
- Store fresh eggplant in fridge for a few days

Friends:

- Beans
- Peppers
- Tomato
- Potato

Enemies:

- None

Did you know? Eggplant has the highest concentration of nicotine of any plant. But don't worry, 20 pounds of eggplant contains only as much nicotine as one cigarette.

GARLIC

Though garlic is one of the smelliest vegetables, the flavor that it adds to any decadent meal is worth it. You can even eat the greens from particular hardneck varieties in salads or garlic pesto. This crop is a great addition to any garden as it is an excellent companion to many plants and deters a number of pests.

Popular Varieties:

- Hardneck
- Softneck

Soil:

- Cultivate deep, rich soil
- Sandy loam is the best type of soil for root vegetables
- Ensure that your bed has appropriate drainage

Planting:

- Plant garlic from bulb in fall for best yield.
- With tips pointing towards the sky, plant individual cloves 2 inches deep
- Space cloves 4 to 6 inches apart for optimal growth
- Cover with a light layer of soil and mulch

Light:

- Grow in full sun

Growing:

- Keep the soil slightly damp throughout the growing season
- Weed often by hand but be sure not to dislodge the delicate bulbs
- Ensure that you do not overwater, as this can cause the plants to rot

Threats:

- Aphid
- White rot
- Thrip
- Nematode

Harvesting:

- Once leaves begin to turn brown, keep an eye on your garlic plants as they'll soon be ready to harvest
- When bulbs are full size and have wrappers formed around each, pull them gently from the ground with a trowel

Storage:

- Trim roots and neck
- Store garlic in hot, dry, dark place for a few weeks to cure before enjoying
- Garlic can last for up to 3 months on wire racks
- Store garlic cloves in oil or vinegar in jar in refrigerator

Friends:

- Dill
- Beet
- Kale
- Spinach
- Potato
- Carrot
- Eggplant

Enemies:

- Asparagus
- Peas
- Beans
- Sage
- Parsely

Did you know? Slice garlic cloves in half and apply them directly to the skin to clear up difficult acne problems.

KALE

This nutrient-rich vegetable grows best in cooler weather and can tolerate fall frost. Try baking kale chips in the oven by de-ribbing your freshly grown crop and sprinkling the leaves with olive oil, salt and red pepper flakes.

Popular Varieties:

- Red Russian
- Vates
- Winterbor

Soil:

- Cultivate rich soil with fertilizer
- Utilize compost for healthier plants

Planting:

- Plant kale from seed any time in early spring or early fall
- Place seeds in ground a 1/4 inch or 1/2-inch deep
- Water lightly after planting
- Avoid planting when temperatures begin to reach over 80 degrees Fahrenheit

Light:

- Grow in full sun

Growing:

- Thin seedlings after 2 weeks so that they are 8 to 12 inches apart
- Water regularly, but don't overwater, keeping soil moist
- Mulch with straw or grass mulch once plants are established to keep in moisture and control weeds

Threats:

- Cabbage worm
- Flea beetle
- Aphid

Harvesting:

- When the majority of the leaves reach the size of your hand, you should begin harvesting
- Collect kale regularly, harvesting a fistful at a time
- Do not pick the terminal bud at the top of the plant in order to lengthen the growing season
- You should be able to harvest again within the week

Storage:

- Keep leaves in airtight plastic bags in the refrigerator for up to 1 week

Friends:

- Beet
- Celery
- Cucumber
- Onion
- Potato

Enemies:

- Beans
- Strawberry
- Tomato

 Did you know? One cup of milk and one cup of kale have the same amount of calcium.

LETTUCE

This versatile, leafy green can be grown in containers or any other small planting area. It is ideal for salad lovers who want to cultivate their own bountiful garden harvest. This crop is incredibly hearty and easy-to-grow with the proper care and nutrients. Sow early enough to prevent your lettuce from bolting in the bright sun and hot weather.

Popular Varieties:

- Iceberg
- Romaine
- Butterhead
- Red deer tongue

- Ithaca
- Sangria
- Lolla Rossa

Soil:

- Cultivate a humus-rich, moisture-retentive soil
- Ensure that your planting area is well-drained so that it is moist without being soggy
- Make sure that there are no large clumps of soil or rocks
- Fertilize soil prior to planting

Planting:

- Start from seed as soon as the ground is no longer frozen
- Plant seeds a 1/4 inch apart in rows 1 1/2 inches apart
- Cover the seeds with a 1/2 inch of light soil
- Water lightly after planting
- Sow additional seeds throughout the growing season for continual harvest

Light:

- Grow in part sun

Growing:

- Thin when seedlings have 4 leaves to 14 to 16 inches apart
- Keep soil surface moist but not soggy so as not to disturb roots
- Water 1 inch per week or any time the leaves begin to wilt, at the base of the plant to prevent mold
- Do not pull weeds, but rather suffocate them with a heavy layer of nutrient-rich mulch
- Lettuce is susceptible to bolting, plant in the shade of taller plants to prevent this

Threats:

- Aphid
- Earwig
- Cutworm
- White mold
- Rabbit
- Slugs

Harvesting:

- Harvest in the early morning to preserve crispness
- Simply pinch off outer leaves and allow young, immature leave to continue to develop
- Check garden every day, as overgrown lettuce is bitter and tasteless
- You can keep harvesting until leaves stop growing or become bitter

- Store lettuce in plastic
  bag in crisper for up to 10
  days before enjoying, but
  it is best eaten fresh

Friends:

- Beet
- Carrot
- Cucumber
- Onion
- Strawberry
- Chive
- Garlic

Enemies:

- Barley
- Broccoli
- Wheat
- Rye

 Did you know? Place recently wilted lettuce in a bowl of ice water for 15 minutes to restore freshness.

ONIONS

No culinary masterpiece is complete without the rich flavor of onions. This cool-season crop does well when planted with most crops and is great for filling in corners of beds to take up space and utilize garden area.

Popular Varieties:

- Yellow sweet Spanish
- Stuttgarter
- Sweet onions
- Egyptian
- Chives
- Shallots

Soil:

- It is best to begin fertilization in early fall to prepare rich soil for optimal onion growth
- Till in aged manure or compost
- Cultivate loose, well-drained, rich soil

Planting:

- Plant onions from seed in early spring, 4 to 6 weeks before last expected frost
- Sow seeds thickly in rows a 1/2 inch deep, cover with light layer of soil but don't pack down
- Try sowing onion seeds with radish seeds to lure root maggots away from onions

Light:

- Grow in full sun

Growing:

- Onions started from seed can take up to 4 months to reach full maturity
- Thin seedlings to 1 inch apart once growth has started
- Thin again in 4 weeks to 6 inches apart

- Keep beds well weeded, using a sharp hoe. Avoid pulling up or digging by hand to prevent damage to roots
- Cover in thick layer of mulch to dissuade weeds and retain moisture
- Water about 1 inch per week. Using soaker hoses or trench watering is most effective.
- Cut or pull out any stalks that have begun to flower. This means they have bolted and are past harvest time

Threats:

- Thrip
- Onion maggot
- Smut
- Japanese beetle
- White rot

Harvesting:

- Once tops turn yellow, bend plants over with edge of rake
- Allow bulbs to rest horizontally on the soil for about one day to continue maturing process
- Loosen soil to ensure proper drying
- When tops finally turn brown, pull up bulbs and let them dry out in the sun

Storage:

- Before storing onions, allow them to dry out completely on wire rack or elevated screen
- Clip tops 1 inch from bulb
- Store in root cellar, or other cool, dry place protected from the sun
- Properly dried bulbs will keep for up to 1 year

Friends:

- Lettuce
- Pepper
- Spinach
- Strawberry
- Tomato

Enemies:

- Beans
- Asparagus
- Peas
- Sage

 Did you know? Eating fresh parsley can help get rid of onion breath.

PARSNIP

Try sauteed parsnips with honey and carrots for a delicious side dish that is sure to satisfy, or add them to soups and stews as a carrot replacement. Though this crop takes a while to mature, the flavor of this root is more than worth the wait.

Popular Varieties:

- Avonresister
- Cobham improved marrow
- Gladiator

Soil:

- Remove any large clods of soil or rocks from planting area and loosen soil 12 to 15 inches
- Prepare soil by tilling in 2 to 3 inches of compost
- Be sure to avoid nitrogen-heavy nutrients

Planting:

- Sow from seed in spring or early summer
- Soak seeds for a few hours to encourage germination
- Place seeds 1/2 inch to 1-inch deep and cover with a light layer of fine compost
- Sow seeds thickly to ensure maximum success

Light:

- Grow in full sun to partial sun

Growing:

- It may take up to 3 weeks for seedlings to emerge, so be patient
- Thin seedlings to 3 to 6 inches apart
- Lightly mulch to conserve moisture
- Weed often by hand, making sure not to disturb roots
- Water regularly

Threats:

- Aphid
- Leafminer
- Carrot rust fly
- Parsnip canker

Harvesting:

- Harvest after hard frost for the best flavor
- Pull or dig up from the ground just as you would with carrots
- Mulch thick or cover with hay and leave in the ground throughout the winter, harvesting as you need

Storage:

- Store parsnips in a cool, dark place for optimal flavor
- Wrap in paper towel, and store in vegetable drawer in crisper for up to 2 weeks

Friends:

- Garlic
- Onions
- Potato
- Rashish

Enemies:

- Carrot
- Celery

 Did you know? Parsnips were used as a natural sweetening agent before sugarcane was introduced to Europe.

PEANUTS

These delicious legumes are mostly a warm, southern crop, but can be planted in the north when started inside before the last frost date. Enjoy peanuts roasted with salt or fresh from the vine.

Popular Varieties:

- Jumbo Virginia
- Early Spanish

Soil:

- Cultivate loose, fertile soil with good drainage for best results

Planting:

- Plant a few weeks after the last frost date in the spring
- Peanut seeds come in shells and can be planted hulled or unhulled
- Sow seeds outside around date of last expected frost
- Space seeds 2 inches deep and 5 inches apart in rows 2 to 3 inches apart
- Firmly pat down soil and water well

Light:

- Grow in full sun

Growing:

- Thin plants to 10 inches apart once sprouted
- When plants are 1 inch tall, hill earth around base of each plant
- Lay down a light mulch, such as straw or grass clippings to prevent soil from crusting
- Water 1 inch per week
- Weed carefully by hand

Threats:

- Corn earworm
- Cutworm
- Potato leafhopper

Harvesting:

- Harvest peanuts before frost, when leaves begin to yellow
- Dig out entire plant with spading fork, shake off most of the soil, then hang indoors to dry for 1 month

Storage:

- Spread peanuts on shallow trays to cure in a warm, dry place for a minimum of 3 weeks
- Peanuts can be stored shelled in airtight containers for short periods or in the freezer for longer periods
- Road nuts at 300 degrees Fahrenheit for 20 minutes before eating

Friends:

- Beet
- Carrot
- Potato
- Lettuce
- Snow pea

Enemies:

- Corn
- Onion

 Did you know? It takes about 540 peanuts to make a 12-ounce jar of peanut butter.

PEAS

Crisp peas define early spring, these green vegetables greeting the motivated gardener with their sweet taste. This annual crop produces a bountiful harvest with the proper temperatures, as the growing season for successful peas is rather short. Boil or steam peas with butter or salt for optimal flavor.

Popular Varieties:

- Snowbird
- Sugar Ann
- Green arrow
- Dakota
- Snap peas

Soil:

- Cultivate well-drained, humus-rich soil
- In the fall before planting, till garden area and mulch with compost
- Do not add more fertilizer before planting. Nitrogen-heavy peas already supply much of their own nutrients and too much nitrogen can produce flowers and not a lot of peas.

Planting:

- Plant seeds in spring 4 to 6 weeks before last expected frost date
- Place seeds 1 inch deep and 2 inches apart
- Cover with a light layer of soil and moisten slightly

Light:

- Grow in full sun to part sun

Growing:

- Water sparsely to prevent flooding but do not let plants dry out
- With vining varieties, you need to provide a trellis or pole for plants to grow up
- Gently hand pull any weeds to ensure that roots are not damaged
- Add 2 inches of heavy mulch to keep roots cool and retain moisture

Threats:

- Aphid
- Mexican bean beetle
- Woodchuck
- Fusarium wilt
- Bacterial blight

Harvesting:

- Peas should be ready to pick about 3 weeks after plant blossoms. They are ready to harvest when plump and bright green
- Cut off pea pods with scissors regularly to encourage more growth
- Harvest in the morning right after dew has dried for fullest flavor

Friends:

- Cucumber
- Beans
- Carrot
- Turnip

Enemies:

- Garlic
- Onion
- Potato

Storage:

- Blanch shelled peas before freezing
- Fresh peas can be kept in the refrigerator for up to 5 days. Place in paper bag and wrap with plastic

 Did you know? The world record for eating peas is held by Janet Harris of Sussex who, in 1984, ate 7,175 peas one by one in 60 minutes using chopsticks!

PEPPERS

There are innumerable pepper varieties with flavors that range from sweet to intense spice. This warm season crop is great for adding color and excitement to any garden. Try stir-frying peppers with the rest of your vegetable harvest and serve on a bed of rice and chicken.

Popular Varieties:

- Bell
- Banana
- Jalapeño
- Vidi
- Olympus

Soil:

- Keep soil well drained to prevent root rot
- Before transplanting, introduce fertilizer or aged compost into your garden soil

Planting:

- Sow seeds 2 months before last expected frost date inside of peat pots
- Keep seedlings moist while indoors and provide at least 5 hours of sunlight
- Once seedlings are 2 to 3 inches tall, thin them by leaving the strongest plant in the pot and cutting off the others at soil level
- Transplant on a cloudy day to reduce danger of sun scorch
- Space transplants 1.5 feet apart in rows 2 feet apart

Light:

- Grow in full sun

Growing:

- Spread a thick layer of light mulch around plants
- Keep plants watered well to avoid bitter peppers
- Pull weeds gently by hand to prevent root damage

Threats:

- Aphid
- Flea beetle
- Cucumber mosaic virus
- Blossom end rot
- Colorado potato beetle

Harvesting:

- Cut peppers from the plant, avoid twisting or pulling
- Wait until bell peppers have matured to red or yellow before harvesting. With other peppers, harvest once they have reached desired size

Storage:

- Freeze peppers in airtight storage bags
- Place in plastic bags in refrigerator for up to 10 days
- Hot varieties are best stored dried or pickled. Pull entire plant from roots and hang it upside down until dry

Friends:

- Basil
- Carrot
- Eggplant
- Onion
- Parsely
- Tomato

Enemies:

- Fennel
- Kohlrabi

 Did you know? Though most people think of them as vegetables, peppers are technically fruits because they are produced from a flowering plant and contain seeds.

POTATOES

This hardy, versatile crop is a staple for any home garden. Boil them, mash them, bake them or cut and season your freshly grown potatoes for a superb snack that is sure to satisfy. This vegetable is incredibly easy to grow and is an excellent way to reap the benefits of your labor all year round.

Popular Varieties:

- Irish Cobbler
- Viking
- Chieftain
- Elba
- Rose gold

Soil:

- Cultivate fertile well-drained soil
- Mix in manure or compost

Planting:

- Plant potatoes zero to 2 weeks after last frost
- Start from seed potatoes, cut into pieces that each contain 2 to 3 eyes
- Wait 2 days before planting cut tubers to give them time to heal
- Place potato pieces in 6-inch wide and 8-inch deep trench every 14 inches, cut side down
- Cover with 3 inches light soil

Light:

- Grow in full sun

Growing:

- As potato vines begin to grow, keep covering with soil, mulched leaves or compost, leaving only a small portion of the vine exposed to the elements. Hilling prevents letting the plants become exposed to sunlight
- Once plants begin to blossom, stop hilling and cover in thick mulch to retain moisture and prevent weeds
- Water thoroughly during times of low rain

Threats:

- Speckle leaf
- Aphid
- Colorado potato beetle
- Blackleg
- Cabbage looper
- Potato scab

Harvesting:

- When plants start to blossom, the earliest tubers, surrounding the base of the plants, are ready to be harvested
- As soon as foliage withers, all potatoes are ready for harvest, so dig plants up before first frost
- Avoid bruising or puncturing tubers

Storage:

- Store freshly harvested potatoes in cool, dry place, brushing off any loose soil
- Only wash right before use. Washing earlier can reduce shelf life
- Potatoes can be stored in root cellar or climate-controlled basement for up to 12 months

Friends:

- Cabbage
- Corn
- Marigold

Enemies:

- Cucumber
- Pea
- Pumpkin
- Raspberry
- Spinach
- Tomato

 Did you know? Grated potatoes are often used to soothe sunburnt skin.

RADISH

These delicious vegetables are incredibly gratifying to grow as they are ready to harvest in under a month after planting. Radish has a mild to hot peppery flavor and a crunchy texture. It is often consumed raw in salads, but it also can be pickled, boiled and fried.

Popular Varieties:

- Rat tail radish pods
- Burpee white
- French breakfast

Soil:

- Work aged manure or compost into the soil
- Cultivate well-drained soil

Planting:

- Plant radish seeds 4 to 6 weeks before the last expected frost, or before the first frost in late summer
- Sow seeds directly into the ground, a 1/2-inch deep and 1 inch apart
- Plant consecutively every 2 weeks while weather is cool for a continual harvest

Light:

- Grow in full sun

Growing:

- After plants have sprouted, thin to 2 inches to prevent overcrowding
- Keep soil moist but be sure not to overwater
- Mulch heavily to keep down weeds and retain moisture

Threats:

- Cabbage maggot
- Clubroot

Harvesting:

- Radishes are fast-growing and can be ready to harvest as soon as 3 weeks after planting
- When you begin to see the top of the radish poking up through the soil and it is about 1 inch in diameter, the radishes are ready to harvest
- Pull straight up on leafy greens and shake off excess soil

Storage:

- Cut the tops off, wash and store the radishes in a plastic bag in the refrigerator for up to 10 days
- Store radish greens separately for up to 3 days

Friends:

- Peas
- Leaf lettuce
- Tomato
- Peppers

Enemies:

- Cauliflower
- Cabbage
- Brussels sprouts
- Turnip

 Did you know? Radishes, onions and garlic were given as wages to the ancient Egyptians who built the pyramids.

RHUBARB

Pick a spot for your rhubarb patch that you will want to continue growing in, as this long-lived perennial can continue production indefinitely. As long as rhubarb has cool enough weather and deep ground freezes, you can enjoy this tart, yet sweet crop in jams and jellies for years to come.

Popular Varieties:

- Victoria
- Canada red
- Valentine
- MacDonald

Soil:

- Cultivate soil that is well-drained and fertile
- Till in manure, fertilizer, compost and other nutrient-heavy organic materials

Planting:

- Grow rhubarb from root divisions as soon as the ground is workable in early spring
- Dig large holes and place the stalks about 4 feet apart and 1 to 2 inches beneath the surface. Plant 3 feet deep for crowns with mature roots
- Mix dislodged soil with compost and manure and pack back into hole around rhubarb to 2 inches within top of hole
- Tamp down soil firmly and water well

Light:

- Grow in full sun

Growing:

- Mulch with a thick layer of straw and cow manure to reduce weeds and retain moisture and nutrients
- Water often, ensuring sufficient moisture
- Mulch again in fall when foliage dies to protect roots from intense freezes
- Remove flower stalks before they bloom to encourage leaf-stalk production

Threats:

- Crown rot
- Cabbage worm
- Verticillium wilt

Harvesting:

- When leaves are fully developed in spring, twist and pull stalks from the crowns
- Do not harvest any rhubarb the first year. In the second year, pick only stalks that are 1 inch thick and only for 1 to 2 months. In the third year, harvest as much as you desire

Friends:

- Garlic
- Onion
- Kale
- Cabbage
- Broccoli

Enemies:

- Potato
- Turnip
- Carrot

Storage:

- Simply wrap rhubarb stalks loosely in foil and they will keep for longer
- You can use this crop for jams and jellies to take advantage of the bountiful harvest

 Did you know? The green leaves from the rhubarb plant are poisonous and should never be eaten.

SPINACH

Spinach is one of the best sources of vitamin A, B and C, and is incredibly resistant to frost and cold temperatures, making it a valuable addition to any garden. This plant produces large yields for delicious salads and can be cooked in many different ways.

Popular Varieties:

- Giant nobel
- Winter bloomsdale
- Tyee
- Malabar spinach

Soil:

- Till soil with aged manure about a week before planting
- Ensure that your soil is well-drained and nitrogen-rich
- Loosen to 1 foot deep before planting

Planting:

- Start from seed as soon as the soil can be worked in spring or 6 weeks before frost in fall
- Sow seeds heavily a 1/2 inch to 1 inch deep, covering with a light layer of soil in beds or rows
- Plant successively throughout the growing season to extend harvest time

Light:

- Grow in full-partial sun

Growing:

- Thin seedling to 4 to 6 inches once they have two true leaves
- To prevent bolting, do not plant when temperatures begin to rise
- Water frequently, even up to 2 times per day to keep soil cool, but do not allow soil to get soggy
- Spread a light layer of mulch, hay, straw or grass clippings to prevent weeds. Do not pull weeds by hand as this can damage the fragile roots

Threats:

- Aphid
- Beet leafhopper
- Cabbage looper
- Curly top
- Downy mildew
- Leaf spot
- Spinach blight

Harvesting:

- Spinach is usually ready to harvest in 6 to 8 weeks from planting date
- Harvest from any plant that has at least 6 leaves 3 to 4 inches long
- Pinch or cut leaves rather than pulling, as this can damage the plants
- If you wait too long to harvest, leaves can become bitter

Storage:

- Cut leaves in thick strops to freeze or dry
- Blanch for 5 minutes before drying or 2 minutes before freezing
- Spinach leaves are best eaten fresh but can be stored in plastic bag in refrigerator for a few days

Friends:

- Beans
- Cabbage
- Kale
- Broccoli
- Celery
- Onion
- Peas

Enemies:

- Potato

 Did you know? Spinach boosts your brainpower, but it can hinder iron absorption. To absorb the iron better, eat spinach with orange slices.

SQUASH AND ZUCCHINI

There are many varieties of squash and zucchini, so do some research to find out what suits your climate and growing need best. Most squash plants need lots of room and plenty of warm temperatures. They also must be harvested before the frost to prevent damage.

Popular Varieties:

- Goldbar
- Cocozelle
- Butterbush
- Cream of the crop

- Summer squash
- Winter squash
- Acorn squash

Soil:

- Warm soil with black plastic in early spring, as squash is very sensitive to cold weather
- Cultivate moist, well-drained soil
- Work compost and manure into soil before planting

Planting:

- Plant squash 1 week after last spring frost
- Sow seeds 1 inch deep and 2 to 3 feet apart in rows
- Certain varieties may do better when planted in hills, with 3 to 4 seeds sown closely together and cultivated with rich soil and compost

Light:

- Grow in full sun

Growing:

- Mulch with light layer of soil to discourage weeds, and retain moisture and nutrients
- Water diligently throughout growing period, at least 1 inch per week at base of plants
- Train squash vines on trellis or pole to save space
- Pull weeds by hand when plants are young, then suppress weeds with heavy organic cover
- When vines have reached 5 feet, pinch off growing tips to encourage fruit-bearing side shoots
- Keep squash and zucchini off the ground to prevent rot. Let it rest on mulch or straw so moisture doesn't get trapped beneath the harvest

Threats:

- Squash vine borer
- Squash bug
- Cucumber beetle
- Stink bug
- Aphids

Harvesting:

- Pick zucchini when it is 6 to 8 inches long
- Harvest summer squash varieties when small and tender, 1 week after flowering
- Cut gourds off vine rather than breaking off
- Harvest winter squash when rind is hard and deep in color

Storage:

- Store fresh summer squash in refrigerator for up to 10 days before enjoying
- Winter squash can be stored in cool, dark places for up to 3 months
- Summer squash tastes delicious when canned, frozen, dried or pickled
- Dry all squash types in the sun until the stems shrivel and turn grey

Friends:

- Celery
- Corn melon

Enemies:

- Potato
- Pumpkin

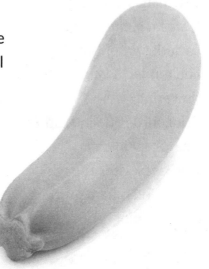

Did you know? Squash blossoms can be fried in a light batter for a delicious treat.

SWEET POTATO

Sweet potatoes grow wonderfully in pots or raised beds on a patio, and don't take up a lot of space when cultivated properly. This warm-season vegetable is rich in nutrients and low in calories. Not to mention, sweet potato fries are absolutely delicious.

Popular Varieties:

- Centennial
- Jewel
- Bunch porto rico
- Stokes
- Georgia jet

Soil:

- Cultivate light, nutrient-rich soil
- Ensure that the soil is light and well-tilled

Planting:

- Plant sweet potatoes from "slips" or root sprouts in early spring, 3 weeks after the last frost
- Before planting, embed slips in soil for 90 days keeping soil warm and moist
- When slips are 6 to 12 inches tall, they are ready to be planted outside
- Cover beds with black plastic to ensure warm soil temperatures
- Make holes 6 inches deep, and 12 inches apart. Bury slips up to top leaves and gently but firmly pack down soil
- Water thoroughly

Light:

- Grow in full sun

Growing:

- Hoe beds occasionally to keep weeds down, making sure not to disturb delicate roots
- Water frequently, keeping soil wet but not soggy. Do not let water sit in bed as this can cause rot
- Mulch 2 weeks after planting to prevent weeds and conserve moisture
- Handle plants as little as possible to prevent damage

Threats:

- Black rot
- Flea beetle
- Nematode
- Weevil
- Sweet potato scurf
- White blister

Harvesting:

- Sweet potatoes will generally be ready to harvest 3 to 4 months after planting
- When the leaves on the end of the vine have started turning yellow, potatoes can be harvested
- Use a spade to gently dig up potatoes, being careful not to puncture potato skins
- Shake off excess dirt but do not wash

Storage:

- To cure, keep potatoes in a warm place at high humidity for 10 to 14 days
- Make sure that potatoes don't touch each other while curing
- Tubers should last for 6 months if cured properly

Friends:

- Parsnip
- Beet
- Bush bean
- Pole bean

Enemies:

- Squash

Did you know? Over 260 billion pounds of sweet potatoes are produced globally every year, making it one of the most important food crops in the world.

TOMATOES

Tomatoes are delicate, but once you have mastered the technique, they are easy to grow. They can even be grown inside in pots throughout the winter. Since you need to harvest all tomatoes before the first frost, you may have green tomatoes leftover that will taste delicious when dipped in egg, flour, black pepper and fried in a skillet.

Popular Varieties:

- New girl
- First lady II
- Amish Paste
- Brandywine

- Matt's wild cherry
- Jet star
- Celebrity

Soil:

- Cultivate well-drained soil
- Mix in aged manure or compost to 1 foot

Planting:

- 6 to 8 weeks before last frost date, sow tomatoes by seed indoors
- Place seeds a 1/4 inch deep and 1 inch apart
- Harden off transplants 1 weeks before planting outside
- Transplant after last spring frost
- Plant seedlings 2 feet apart
- Water well to reduce transplant shock

Light:

- Grow in full sun

Growing:

- Establish tomato cages or trellises
- Lay down a deep mulch to smother weeds and conserve moisture
- Water at least 1 inch per week as base of plant
- Prune plants by picking off suckers so that only a couple of stems are growing per stake

Threats:

- Aphids
- Flea beetles
- Tomato hornworm
- Whiteflies
- Blossom-end rot

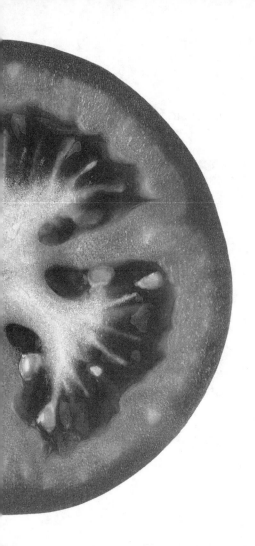

Harvesting:

- Leave tomatoes on the vine as long as possible
- Cut or gently twist off at the vine
- Pick when fruit is evenly red but still warm

Storage:

- Never refrigerate fresh tomatoes
- Core fresh tomatoes and place in freezer-safe bags to freeze
- To ripen green tomatoes, wrap them in newspaper and place them in a cool, dark area

Friends:	**Enemies:**

Friends:
- Carrot
- Celery
- Chive
- Cucumber
- Melon
- Onion
- Peas
- Peppers

Enemies:
- Corn
- Dill
- Fennel
- Potato
- Walnut

 Did you know? You can ease a headache by drinking tomato juice blended with fresh basil.

"Gardening is the art that uses flowers and plants as paint and the soil and sky as canvas."

— Elizabeth Murray

Fruit Growing Tips

Adding fruit to your garden is such a treat! Here are a few tips to get you started.

Selection

A wide variety of fruit-bearing trees and bushes can be grown, regardless of size, as long as they are compatible with your climatic conditions. If you have ample space, large fruit trees not only provide enough fruit for your needs and some to spare, but make great additions to the landscape. When space is at a premium, train regular trees into espaliers or choose the newly developed dwarf trees that can be grown even in containers. Their yield may be considerably less, but still sufficient to meet your needs.

Many commercial fruit varieties are freely available in nurseries. They are specially chosen for their attractive color, size and quality, rather than taste and flavor. Apples, pears, plums, cherries, nectarines, apricots, strawberries and blueberries are popular choices, but easily perishable soft fruits like mulberries, currants, salmonberries and gooseberries are worth growing for their flavorful results.

Be sure to buy named cultivars and grafts from reputed suppliers. Check whether they are self-pollinating as you may need to grow more than one plant of self-sterile types to ensure cross-pollination and a good fruit set.

Location

Fruit trees are long-term investments, so they should also be placed in your garden or yard with care. Saplings may be small, but their final size should be taken into consideration when planting them. Many fruit trees look good in ornamental gardens, especially apple and cherry trees that put up a delightful flower show in spring.

 I love using fruit trees as a focal point in my garden and plant a variety of shade-loving plants underneath. Blackberry, raspberry and blueberry bushes make good hedges and can be used for separating different areas in your garden. Strawberry patches need to be relocated every few years.

Fruit trees and bushes are ideally grown where they are easily accessible, but planting them too close to your house can create a few problems during the flowering season when pollinators make a beeline for nectar. Fallen fruit littering the ground can be another problem. The juice of mulberries and others, when crushed underfoot, can stain hardwood floors. Nevertheless, a clear view of the orchard from your home can alert you to birds and rodents stealing fruit. I like to keep a few dwarf trees in containers on and around my patio. They add great interest and can be easily harvested.

Sun exposure

Most fruit trees need full sun in order to produce good yields. An exception is sour cherries; they do pretty well espaliered on a north-facing wall. Unlike sweet cherries, they don't need sun to sweeten the fruit. Pears can tolerate partial shade for part of the day, although they do need a few hours of sunshine to produce a good crop. Plum trees like some protection from hot afternoon sun, but require full sun in the morning.

Most bushes bearing soft fruit can do well in filtered light and partial to full shade during part of the day. Gooseberries and redcurrants reliably produce in shady locations, but the bushes growing in full sun give sweeter berries. Raspberries, blackcurrants and blueberries do not disappoint even in partial shade. Strawberry patches thrive in full sun, but a bit of afternoon shade is often welcome, especially in places with hot summers. Alpine strawberries are excellent for shady areas; these everbearing plants are low maintenance and produce flavorful berries.

Planting

Fruit trees are best planted in early spring in areas with cold, freezing winters. When the young trees are planted as soon as the ground thaws, they'll take off almost immediately, growing new roots and leaves. In areas with milder winters, fall planting is preferred because the plants are allowed time to concentrate on growing new roots before they have to put out leaves in spring. Trees in nursery containers can wait, but bare-root trees that become available in fall should be planted as soon as they arrive, but not when the weather is foul.

Begin by preparing a planting hole that's double the size of the root ball. Ease out the root ball as gently as possible and direct the roots towards the periphery of the hole and fill with soil. Resist the temptation to plant the tree deeper than it was in its original pot. Grafted trees should have a slightly swollen graft site above the ground. Tie the tree to a sturdy support to keep it upright and stable.

Watering

Newly planted trees and bushes should be watered as soon as they are planted to prevent the roots from drying out. Continue watering every day for at least three weeks after planting, and then gradually reduce the frequency which will  encourage the trees to spread their roots into the surrounding areas. You should also place mulch around the tree base, a few inches away from the trunk, to help keep moisture in and reduce soil temperature fluctuations. Constant moisture from the mulch can initiate stem rot.

Young trees may need weekly watering for the first two to three years, especially in the summer. Water deeply so that moisture seeps into the lower layers of soil and encourages the roots to grow downward. If you have several new trees, consider setting up a drip irrigation system, but provide multiple emitters per tree, spreading them out in a wide circle around the tree.

Fertilizing

When you set young trees, be sure to backfill the holes with compost mixed with the garden soil which will take care of most of their nutritional requirements for some time. Adding chemical fertilizers now might burn the roots and kill the tree.

In the spring, apply a balanced organic fertilizer. Remove the mulch from around the tree base and water the tree before loosening the soil with a garden fork and mixing the fertilizer into the soil, taking care to avoid direct contact with the stem. Cover the base with fresh mulch and water thoroughly to help dilute the fertilizer and prevent root burn.

Organic fertilizers like bone meal, blood meal and fish meal have a lasting effect, so frequent application is unnecessary. Compost tea is excellent as a growth promoter.

Pruning

Pruning fruit trees is somewhat of an art that I have learned through the ages. It is not something to go into without a bit of an education, as pruning in the wrong way at the wrong time can harm trees and hurt your harvest.

Different pruning and shaping conventions exist for different fruit trees but all are geared towards maximizing light exposure for all the branches and promoting air circulation. Limiting tree height and crowded branches for easy harvesting is another goal.

Fall planted trees can be pruned the following spring, but allow spring-planted trees more time, waiting until early summer. Remove low-lying branches and narrow-angled ones; vertical branches, called waterspouts, and those growing close together or towards the center of the tree have to go. All these cuts should be made flush with the trunk, with the remaining branches shortened by one-third, cutting them off just above an outward-facing bud. Fruit bushes can be pruned to the ground the first year to encourage the growth of long, healthy canes that can be trained and pruned further.

Always use sharp pruning tools, disinfecting them with isopropyl alcohol to avoid introducing pathogens into the cuts. Repeat the disinfection process every time you move to the next tree or bush.

Pollination

You should welcome bees and other pollinating insects to your garden in order to maximize fruit production. Most plants carry male and female parts in the same flower or have male flowers and female flowers on the same plant. Many such plants, including peaches, nectarines and some citrus plants, are self-pollinating, with female parts accepting pollen from the same plant. But cross-pollination often increases fruit set.

Some strictly cross-pollinating plants do not set fruit unless the female flowers receive pollen from another compatible plant whether they carry male flowers in the same plant or have separate male and female plants. Apples, sweet cherries, plums and pears are mostly cross-pollinating and require a suitable pollinizer companion to be planted not too far off. Some self-pollinating varieties are also available, so you might want to check with your local nursery before purchasing the plants.

If you don't find enough pollinating insects visiting your fruit trees in flower, hand pollination is an option. Although time-consuming, it is not difficult; all you have to do is transfer the pollen from one flower to the stigma of another using a paintbrush. This can be quite practical for dwarf fruit trees.

Fruit Thinning

Fruit thinning can give you better quality fruit, because removing some fruit encourages the growth of the remaining ones. The idea is to have a higher leaf-to-fruit ratio that supports the growth of good-sized fruits. Apples, pears, peaches and plums respond well to thinning, which is usually done by hand.

It's obviously harder to hand-thin smaller fruit like cherries and gooseberries. To make it easier, you can remove smaller branches that lie in the shade to reduce the total load. Large, flavorful fruit develop from flowers that get full sun. Some gardeners prefer to do flower thinning, but it is riskier since there's no guarantee that the remaining flowers will develop into fruit.

Fruit thinning should be done as early as possible because it gives the fruit more time to develop with a favorable leaf-to-fruit ratio. Standard ratio for apple trees is 40:1, which means there should be 40 leaves for every fruit. A higher ratio of 75:1 is ideal for peaches. Dwarf fruit trees can do with fewer leaves per fruit because their leaves get better sun exposure.

Harvesting

Generally, fruit ripened on the tree or bush has the best flavor and sweetness, but some types of fruit have to be harvested before they reach their full maturity. It's important to aim for the right balance between sweetness and crispness because fully ripe fruit has poor keeping quality. Color and aroma of the fruit may give some indication of their ripeness, but tasting a few samples from the tree is the best way to determine the right time for harvesting.

Apples and pears should be picked when they're still firm to touch, but also sweet to taste. Cherries and gooseberries meant for cooking can be gathered slightly unripe, but wait until the plums are slightly softer. Most fruits will come away easily when they're ready, so you can pluck a few at a time. However, fruits falling from the tree does not always mean they're ripe. Still, if a windfall happens, there's no point in waiting.

Storing and Preserving

If you have good sized fruit trees and several bushes, you're likely to get more fruit than you can use at once. Enjoy them in the offseason by storing them in a refrigerator or a fruit cellar. You can harvest the fruits when they're slightly under-ripe if you intend to store them for a long time. Special care should be taken to avoid damaging the fruit while harvesting, otherwise it will decay quickly. Wash the fruit gently before refrigerating as soon as you harvest.

Apples keep well for three to four months without refrigeration if you keep them in a cool, dark place, plums and pears should be refrigerated. Not all fruits store well, even in the refrigerator. The goodness of strawberries, raspberries and other soft fruits can be enjoyed by preserving them, either by freezing or drying. I like to juice fresh fruit and also make fruit leather using a dehydrator. You can also make jams and jellies out of harvested fruit — just watch for low sugar recipes.

"Everything that slows us down and forces patience, everything that sets us back into the slow circles of nature, is a help. Gardening is an instrument of grace. "

— May Sarton

Let's Get Growing — Fruit

There is nothing more delicious or nutritious than growing your own fruit. Here are my favorite fruit bushes and trees to grow and all the information you need to get started. Have fun!

APPLES

Do some research to make sure that you plant the right apple tree for your climate. Apple growing can be a little tricky, but with patience and effort, you will soon be biting into a crisp piece of fruit straight from your own garden.

Popular Varieties:

- Liberty
- Williams pride
- Honey gold
- Fiesta
- Fuji
- Granny Smith

Soil:

- Cultivate well-drained, rich soil
- Mulch area with straw or hay to keep soil moist and provide nutrients before planting

Planting:

- Apple trees take up a lot of space, with certain varieties reaching up to 30 feet tall. Choose the spot for your trees carefully
- Buy dormant, 1-year-old, unbranched grafted trees
- Plant apples in early spring, 20 to 30 feet apart
- Do not plant near wooded areas or other trees
- Dig a hold 2 times the diameter of the root system and 2 feet deep
- Pat down replaced soil firmly to prevent air pockets

Light:

- Grow in full sun

Growing:

- Healthy trees should grow 8 to 12 inches per year. If this growth does not occur, check to make sure that your soil is providing sufficient levels of potassium, calcium and boron for your saplings
- Mulch yearly with a 2-inch layer of compost
- Prune trees yearly in late winter or early spring, training them to desired shape
- Once tree begins to bear fruit, start thinning by removing the smallest apples in each cluster before they reach 1 inch in diameter. Remaining fruit should be 6 inches apart
- Remove weak twigs and misplaced buds

Threats:

- Apple scab
- Apple maggot
- Cankerworm
- Codling moth
- Baldwin spot
- Canker dieback
- Cedar-apple rust
- Crown gall
- Deer
- Japanese beetles

Harvesting:

- Some apple trees can take 4 to 8 years to produce fruit, so be patient
- Pluck apples when background color is no longer green
- Twist slightly and pull up on ripe fruit

Storage:

- Store apples that you plan to eat soon in a humid refrigerator, as long as they are not rotten
- Wrap individual apples in newspaper on breathable trays in cardboard box

Friends:

- Buckwheat

Enemies:

- Walnut tree
- Potato

Did you know? More than 2,500 varieties of apples are grown in the United States, but only the crabapple is native to North America.

APRICOT

Apricots are a great addition to the orchard. With its sweet, delicate flavor, this orange fruit can be made into a unique pie, or dried and added to trail mix for a high-energy snack. If you live in a dry climate, apricot trees are a good choice as they are one of the most drought-resistant fruit trees.

Popular Varieties:

- Jerseycot
- Harcot
- Harglow

Soil:

- Cultivate light, well-drained soil

Planting:

- Plant seedlings 20 to 25 feet apart
- Dig hole deep and wide enough that the entire root system fits easily into the hole
- Mix peat moss or compost into removed topsoil before returning to hole
- Water tree deeply right away
- Clear away all perennial weeds in growing spot

Light:

- Grow in full sun

Growing:

- Remove blossoms or young fruit so that apricots are 4 inches apart
- Mulch around tree to protect roots from freezes and retain moisture
- Water regularly, as drought is one of the greatest threats to apricot trees

Threats:

- Aphid
- Cankerworm
- Codling moth
- Cherry fruit sawfly
- Bacterial canker
- Bacterial spot
- Black knot

Harvesting:

- Apricots will bear fruit in 4 to 5 years, so patience is necessary
- Twist at stem and pluck from the tree carefully. Avoid damaging delicate fruit

Storage:

- This fruit drys wonderfully in a dehydrator. Split fruit and remove the pit before drying
- Store canned apricots or make into jam or jelly

Friends:

- Alder
- Brambles
- Buckwheat

Enemies:

- Persian melon
- Plumb
- Pepper
- Potato
- Raspberry

 Did you know? The apricot is now cultivated on every continent except Antarctica.

BLACKBERRIES

Blackberries are surprisingly vigorous, so be sure plant them in an area that can be filled with this prolific crop. When cared for properly and pruned effectively, perennial blackberries will return with a bountiful harvest every year.

Popular Varieties:

- Erect thorny - Navaho, Arapaho
- Erect thornless - Cherokee, Brazos
- Trailing - Olallie

Soil:

- Cultivate fertile, well-drained soil
- Blackberries need sandy, loamy soil
- Eradicate perennial weeds from planting area

Planting:

- Space blackberries 3 to 5 feet apart
- Transplant from established plant in very early spring after chance of frost has passed
- Dig a large enough hole so that the roots will fit without bending

Light:

- Grow in full sun

Growing:

- Mulch regularly to suffocate weeds and retain moisture
- Water 1 inch per week. More in season of drought
- Provide trellises to support your brambles
- Pull weeds gently by hand
- After the harvest, cut back vines to soil level

Threats:

- Raspberry borer
- Fruit worm
- Gray mold
- Cane borer
- Mite

Harvesting:

- When berries slide off of vine easily, harvest into small containers. They should be plump and fully black
- Harvest often as blackberries mature quickly
- Be careful when picking berries from the vine, as the thorns can puncture your skin easily

Storage:

- Freeze within two days of harvesting by spreading out on cookie sheet and sticking in freezer
- Store in heavy freezer bags once solid
- Keep in plastic bag in refrigerator for 4 to 7 days

Friends:

- Grape
- Beans
- Peas

Enemies:

- Black walnut

Did you know? During the Civil War, blackberry tea was said to be the best cure for dysentery. Temporary truces were declared throughout the conflict to allow both Union and Confederate soldiers to forage for blackberries.

BLUEBERRIES

Nothing says summer more than blue-stained fingers and plump berries dripping juice down your chin. This delicious perennial is easy to grow and after a few unproductive seasons, will produce more fruit than you could ever eat.

Popular Varieties:

- Highbush
- Lowbush
- Half-high
- Rabbiteye

Soil:

- Cultivate fertile, well-drained soil that is slightly acidic
- Mix in compost or other organic materials

Planting:

- 1 to 3-year-old plants are the best option for successful cultivation
- Plant bushes as soon as ground thaws in spring
- Dig holes 20 inches deep and 18 inches wide
- Space bushes 5 feet apart in rows 8 feet apart

Light:

- Grow in full sun

Growing:

- Mulch regularly to suffocate weeds and retain moisture. Apply a 2-inch layer of pine needles, sawdust or wood chips
- Provide 1 to 2 inches of water per week
- Drape netting over ripening blueberries so that birds will be deterred
- Do not allow fruit to grow for the first 2 years after planting. Pinch off blossoms so that none can develop
- After 4 years, begin the pruning process in late winter or early spring
- Cut out dead, weak, broken or spindly offshoots

- Bacterial canker
- Cane gall
- Crown gall
- Mummy berry
- Blueberry maggot
- Cherry fruit worm

Harvesting:

- Blueberry bushes take up to 6 years to reach full production
- Leave blueberries on the bush 5 to 10 days after they turn blue
- Berries should slide off the bush easily and be slightly soft and sweet
- Harvest often as blueberries mature quickly
- Harvest directly into container and handle as little as possible so that protective wax is not removed

Storage:

- Freeze within 2 days of harvesting by spreading out on cookie sheet and sticking in freezer
- Store in heavy freezer bags once solid
- Keep in plastic bag in refrigerator for 4 to 7 days

Friends:

- Basil
- Beans
- Thyme

Enemies:

- None

 Did you know? Blueberry flesh is actually green. Only its skin is blue.

CHERRIES

Not only are fresh cherries totally delicious, and scrumptious when baked into a piping hot pie, but cherry blossoms can brighten up any yard. Be sure to pick the right variety, as trees vary between sweet and tart, to dwarf and full-size.

Popular Varieties:

- Black Tartarian sweet
- Bing sweet
- Stella sweet
- Early Richmond sour
- Montmorency sour
- Meteor sour

Soil:

- Ensure that soil is deep and well-drained

Planting:

- Plant cherries from saplings in late fall or early spring
- Space plants 30 feet apart
- Dig hole deep enough for root ball to fit easily without crushing roots

Light:

- Grow in full-partial sun

Growing:

- Apply thick layer of mulch to retain moisture
- Drape netting over trees to protect from birds. They love cherry trees and will do anything to get to unripe fruit
- Water regularly, especially in dry areas, but be sure not to overwater
- Prune trees every winter to encourage growth

Threats:

- Aphids
- Japanese beetles
- Caterpillars
- Brown rot
- Black knot
- Bacterial canker

Harvesting:

- Wait to pick until fully ripe when tree begins to droop slightly
- Gently pull off clusters, keeping the stems on the fruit. This will keep them fresh longer and help them retain their flavor
- Harvest within a week's time
- Cherries will not produce until the fourth year

Storage:

- Cherries are best eaten fresh
- Make into cherry pie
- If plucked when still firm, cherries are great frozen

Friends:

- Alfalfa
- Bromegrass
- Clover

Enemies:

- None

 Did you know? Archaeologists have discovered fossilized cherry pits in prehistoric caves throughout Europe and Asia.

CITRUS

Just because you live in a cold climate, doesn't mean you can't enjoy your very own citrus trees. Plant dwarf trees in large pots on wheels, rolling them outside on the patio in the warm season and bringing them into a sunny spot in your home during the winter months. These trees provide lovely green foliage and gorgeous colorful fruit to enhance the beauty of your garden. Plus, who doesn't love a glass of fresh cold lemonade or orange juice on a hot summer day?

Popular Varieties:

- Lemon
- Lime
- Grapefruit
- Orange
- Tangerine
- Pummelo
- Kumquat
- Calamondin

Soil:

- Cultivate light, rich, well-drained soil
- Spread compost or well-rotted manure on planting area

Planting:

- Citrus trees should be planted in a sunny, well-protected area
- Unless you live in warm southern states, container gardening is the best option for successful citrus cultivation
- Standard size citrus trees should be planted 12 to 15 feet apart

- If soil is not well-drained, plant trees on a slightly raised mound to prevent waterlogging. Mound should be about 1.5 feet high
- All types of citrus fruit are easily damaged by frost. Limes are generally the most susceptible and kumquats are the least
- Select young, nursery-raised trees. Pick those with fewer fruits and flowers because they have put more energy into sturdy top and root growth
- Plant container-grown trees in spring

Light:

- Grow in full sun

Growing:

- Wrap the trunk with commercial tree wrap or newspaper for the first year, or paint it with diluted white latex paint to prevent sunburn and protect trees
- Water newly planted trees at least once per week for the first year. Never wait until trees begin to wilt to water
- Water slowly and deeply; shallow sprinkling causes more harm than good
- Cover with a thick layer of mulch. Keeping it at least 6 inches away from the trunk
- Most citrus trees require little pruning other than removing dead or broken branches in the dormant season

- Remove suckers as soon as they shoot from the ground
- If there is a threat from frost, cover trees with fabric sheets
- Thin subpar fruit to allow room for other fruit to develop

Threats:

- Aphids
- Spider mites
- Root rot
- Crown rot
- Fungal leaf spots
- Fruit flies

Harvesting:

- Citrus trees bear fruit in 3 to 4 years
- Use taste tests to determine when fruit is ripe, as color can be misleading
- Cut fruit from tree with pruning shears, do not simply pull from tree
- Ripe fruit can stay on tree for up to 3 months

Storage:

- Citrus can be stored in refrigerator for 3 or more weeks

Friends:

- Peas
- Alfalfa
- Yarrow
- Lemon balm
- Parsely

Enemies:

- None

Did you know? Historically, rations of oranges were given to British soldiers on long ocean voyages to prevent scurvy. Scurvy is caused by vitamin C deficiency, so the high vitamin C content in oranges made them perfect for preventing the disease.

CURRANTS

This fruit can be found in black, white, pink and red, with each variety having a slightly different taste and tartness level. Currants are a perennial plant and do well in areas that receive natural moisture and at least one freeze per winter. Experiment with the different types of currants, or plant all of the colors to add variety to your garden.

Popular Varieties:

- European black currant
- American black
- Buffalo
- Ben Sarek

- Titania
- Jonkheer van Tets
- Cascade

Soil:

- Cultivate well-drained, loamy soil
- Work in lots of compost or other organic material, or build raised beds if necessary

Planting:

- Plant currant plants from mid-fall to early spring
- Space currants 5 to 6 feet apart in rows at least 6 feet apart

Light:

- Grow in full sun

Growing:

- Maintain a 2 to 3-inch layer of heavy mulch to retain moisture and suffocate weeds
- Gently hand-pull any weeds that do appear, making sure not to disturb the fragile roots
- Prune annually to allow light and air in

Threats:

- Gooseberry fruit worm
- American gooseberry mildew
- Blister rust

Harvesting:

- Leave berries on bush for a few days to ensure that they are sufficiently ripe
- Pull off entire fruit clusters when ripe, rather than individual berries

Storage:

- Currants don't store well fresh, so eat immediately
- If you do not want to eat right away, use in preserves, jellies or juices
- Freeze in airtight bags for use in smoothies

Friends:

- Gooseberries

Enemies:

- White pine

 Did you know? Oil extracted from the seed of black currants has application in the cosmetic industry. It is mostly used in the manufacture of skin care products.

FIGS

You can utilize your patio to grow potted figs for a beautiful and practical addition to your outdoor living space. Cook figs by simmering them with a dash of lemon and honey for about 20 minutes, mashing them as they cook. Then puree in a food processor or blender. Use frozen puree for ice cream sauce, toast spread or cookie filling.

Popular Varieties:

- Brown turkey
- Chicago
- Celeste
- Kadota
- King

Soil:

- Ensure soil is well-drained and contains plenty of organic material

Planting:

- If you are short on space, you can easily grow figs indoors in containers. Grow them in soil-based potting mix and add fine bark chips
- Plant in early spring
- Plant in a hole that is deeper and wider than the existing root system
- Space tree 20 feet away from any other trees or buildings

Light:

- Plant in full or filtered light if container planting
- Grow in full sun if planting in the ground

Growing:

- It is important to keep tree moist in dry seasons
- Water figs deeply at least once per week
- Apply thick layer of mulch to retain moisture and prevent weeds
- Fig trees require little pruning. Remove dead or broken branches in winter to encourage growth
- To protect fig trees in winter, cover them with a cylindrical cage of hardware cloth filled with straw

Threats:

- Birds
- Nematodes
- Leaf spots
- Rust
- Thrips

Harvesting:

- Figs should be full colored and slightly soft
- Wear gloves or long sleeves when harvesting to protect skin from sap that can cause irritation
- Check for figs daily in growing season

Storage:

- Store in refrigerator for 2 to 3 days
- Freeze whole for later use
- Dry in dehydrator for later use

Friends:

- Strawberries

Enemies:

- None

 Did you know? The early Olympic athletes used figs as a training food. Figs were also presented as laurels to the winners, becoming the first Olympic "medal."

GOOSEBERRIES

Gooseberries are similar to currants in that they come in many colorful varieties. The typical gooseberries are green with light stripes but can be red, yellow, purple, black or white and contain small edible seeds. Each variety also has a slightly different flavor and makes wonderful preserves.

Popular Varieties:

- Invicta
- Poorman
- Captivator

Soil:

- Cultivate well-drained, loamy soil
- Work in lots of compost or other organic material, or build raised beds if necessary

Planting:

- Plant gooseberry plants anytime from late fall-early spring
- Space gooseberries 5 to 6 feet apart in rows at least 6 feet apart
- Water immediately after planting

Light:

- Grow in full sun or partial-dappled shade

Growing:

- Mulch with organic matter to conserve moisture and suppress weeds, maintaining a 2 to 3-inch layer
- In dry spells, water every two weeks. Do not overwater but keep soil evenly moist

- Gently hand-pull any weeds that do appear, making sure not to disturb the fragile roots
- Prune annually to allow light and air in
- Gooseberry plants survive 12 to 15 years with proper care

Threats:

- Gooseberry powdery mildew
- Gooseberry sawfly
- Leaf spot
- Currantworms
- Cane borer

Harvesting:

- Gooseberries ripen over a 2 to 3 week period, so bunches must be picked several times
- Wear gloves to protect your hands from the thorns as you pull off the fruit

Storage:

- All gooseberries freeze well
- Refrigerate in sealed container for up to 2 weeks

Friends:

- Beans
- Tomato
- Chives

Enemies:

- None

 Did you know? One mature gooseberry bush produces 8 to 10 pounds of fruit per season.

GRAPES

You don't have to have a vineyard to cultivate grapes. Start growing your own vines today and preserve your fresh grapes as jelly, juice or wine. Grapes add a lovely element to your garden and can be trained to grow up the side of your house to utilize garden space.

Popular Varieties:

- Edelweiss
- Reliance
- Seibel
- Swenson red
- Magnolia
- Valiant
- Concord
- Niagara

Soil:

- Begin preparing your soil 1 year before you plant grapes
- Eliminate perennial weeds completely
- Add lots of organic matter and ensure that the soil is well-balanced
- Cultivate deep, well-drained and loose soil

Planting:

- Plant dormant, 1-year-old vines in spring before buds begin to open
- Soak roots for 1 to 2 hours before planting in a bucket of water
- Prune each vine to leave 2 leaf buds before planting
- Construct a trellis or cage before planting so vines have a place to grow
- Space vines 6 to 10 feet apart
- Dig hole 12 inches deep and 12 inches wide
- Cover roots with 6 inches of topsoil and tamp down
- Water well at time of planting

Light:

- Grow in full sun

Growing:

- Prune annually when vines are dormant. The more you prune, the more grapes you will have
- In the first year, cut back all except 2 or 3 buds
- Mulch with compost to retain moisture and prevent weeds
- Mesh nets are useful to keep birds from eating grapes

Harvesting:

- If grapes are ripening, pinch back some foliage to let in light
- Grapevines will bear fruit by their third or fourth season
- Harvest when fruit tastes ripe
- Grapes should be rich in color, juicy, full-flavored and plump
- They do not ripen off the vine so be sure that fruit is to your liking

Threats:

- Aphids
- Japanese beetles
- Powdery mildew
- Black rot

Storage:

- Store in cardboard boxes lined with clean straw in root cellar or basement
- Dry in the sun under clear polyethylene until stems shrivel slightly. This shortens drying time and yields raisins

Friends:

- Blackberries

Enemies:

- None

 Did you know? On average, one acre of grapes can produce around 15,000 glasses of wine.

KIWI

Kiwi is an excellent choice for those looking to add a discussion plant to their home garden. Kiwis taste great on ice cream, in preserves, baked goods or on top of yogurt. These ornamental vines require little care and will produce fruit for up to 50 years if pruned properly.

Popular Varieties:

- Arctic beauty
- Chinese kiwis
- Issai
- Hayward
- Raisin kiwi

Soil:

- Cultivate loose, well-drained soil
- Avoid soggy, low areas that will flood roots

Planting:

- Provide trellis, arbor or other sturdy support for vines
- Plant from vines in spring
- Place 10 to 18 feet apart
- Water new plants immediately

Light:

- Grow in full sun and partial shade

Growing:

- Cover with light layer of mulch or other organic compound
- Prune back newly planted vines to 4 to 5 buds
- When these buds grow, select a sturdy shoot to be the main trunk and snip off the others
- Tie it to the support, encouraging it to grow to the top of the arbor
- When it does, cut off the tip to stimulate new growth
- Once a month, per summer, prune all new growth back to 4 or 5 buds
- Prune overgrown vines back severely
- Cover vines if frost threatens in spring or fall

Threats:

- Leaf rollers
- Spider mites
- Thrips
- Japanese beetles
- Nematodes

Harvesting:

- Vines bear in 2 to 3 years
- The fruits will begin to ripen in late summer. They should give a little when pressed with your finger
- Pick them just before they are fully ripe and allow them to soften at room temperature
- Snap off at stem

Storage:

- Kiwis keep in the refrigerator for 2 months before softening
- Fruit keeps on counter for up to 6 weeks

Friends:

- None

Enemies:

- None

 Did you know? Kiwis contain ten times the vitamin C of oranges.

MELON AND CANTALOUPE

While melons may require special effort for maximum yield, their delicious flavor is worth it! Chilled watermelon can complete a backyard summer party, with just the right amount of sweetness to balance out the savory tastes of a BBQ.

Popular Varieties:

- Hale's best jumbo
- Minnesota midget
- Bush star
- Ambrosia
- Athena
- Watermelon
- Honeydew

Soil:

- Till compost or aged manure in the soil before planting
- Cultivate loamy, well-drained soil

Planting:

- Grow vines in raised rows to hold in heat and ensure good drainage
- Plant seeds in spring once temperature warms to at least 65 degrees Fahrenheit
- Place seeds 1 inch deep, 18 inches apart, in rows 3 feet apart

Light:

- Grow in full sun

Growing:

- Vines can be trained to trellis to provide support and save space
- Mulch with black plastic to warm soil and prevent weeds
- Water at base of plant 1 to 2 inches per week
- Thin to 2 to 3 plants per hill
- Handle vines extremely carefully as they're very delicate

Threats:

- Aphids
- Cucumber beetles
- Squash vine borer moths
- Fusarium wilt

Harvesting:

- Vine-ripened fruit should break easily with no pressure on the stem
- Melons will be fragrant when ripe
- If ground surface on a melon has turned from a light straw color to gold, orange or rich yellow, it is ripe

Friends:

- Lettuce
- Radish
- Tansy
- Marigolds

Enemies:

- Potatoes

Storage:

- Melons kept in a cool place can last up to 2 weeks
- If cut, melons will last in the refrigerator for about 3 days

 Did you know? While we now have certified BPA free plastic, stainless steel tumblers and handy thermoses, early explorers used watermelons as canteens.

NECTARINE AND PEACH

Choose peach trees that suit your particular climate, as they are very susceptible to cold weather and need proper fertilization. Also, though you may have thought that they were different plants, the fuzz on peach skins is controlled by a single gene. This means that nectarines and peaches are virtually identical species, not hybrids of each other.

Popular Varieties:

- Redhaven
- Reliance
- Harmony

Soil:

- Cultivate well-drained, fertile soil
- Soil should be sandy-light on the surface with a heavier texture in the subsoil
- Fertilize ground with compost

Planting:

- Avoid planting in low areas because frost can settle there and kill trees
- Plant trees in early spring
- Pick 1-year-old, nursery-raised trees
- Remove plant from its pot and use shears to cut away any root-bound soil
- Dig a hole that is 2 inches deeper and wider than the original pot
- Space trees 15 to 20 feet apart
- Peaches are easily damaged by frost, so choose a site on the upper half of a north-facing slope

Light:

- Grow in full sun

Growing:

- Prune trees annually to encourage production
- Thin so fruits are 8 inches apart on the branch after the tree blooms
- Peach trees should grow 1 to 1.5 feet per year. If growth is slower, correct soil deficiencies
- Ensure even moisture around roots. Drip irrigation may help in keeping soil moist

Threats:

- Borers
- Aphids
- Japanese beetles
- Leafhoppers
- Brown rot
- Powdery mildew
- Leaf curl

Harvesting:

- Peach trees bear fruit within 3 years
- Fruit skin color will change from green to yellow as they ripen. It should give slightly under pressure
- Hold fruit gently and twist off branch, making sure not to bruise the fruit

Storage:

- Store ripe peaches in plastic bag in refrigerator for 1 week
- Store peaches by canning or making preserves such as jam or jelly
- Pickled peaches are also a delicious way of enjoying your harvest
- Freeze for use in smoothies. Peel, put and cut in halves or slices

Friends:

- Alder
- Brambles
- Buckwheat
- Goldenrod
- Strawberry

Enemies:

- None

Did you know? You can skin peaches quickly and neatly by dropping a few at a time into a pot of boiling water for about 30 seconds and then transferring them to cold water immediately. The skins will slip right off in your hand.

PEAR

Pear trees generally require minimal care once established and can survive well in moist, overcast conditions. These trees can survive for 200 to 300 years and can produce healthy fruit for over 100 years. Choose a spot where your pear trees can grow and flourish for a long time.

Popular Varieties:

- Bartlett
- Kieffer
- Anjou
- Magness
- Bose

Soil:

- Cultivate fertile, well-drained, deep soil

ALTERNATIVE DAILY

Planting:

- Plant at least two varieties of pear trees, as they will need to be cross-pollinated to produce fruit
- Space standard-size trees 20 to 25 feet apart
- Remove plant from its pot and use shears to cut away any root bound soil
- Dig a hole that is a few inches wider and deeper than the original pot
- Water immediately after planting

Light:

- Grow in full sun

Growing:

- Water young trees well during dry spells to prevent wilt
- Thin fruit well, leaving 6 inches between each cluster of pears
- Prune trees lightly every year, when tree is dormant and not budding
- Pear trees tend to be slightly more resistant to frost damage than other fruit trees
- Mulch with a thick layer of organic matter and irrigate deeply if the soil dries out

Threats:

- Fire blight
- Pear psylla
- Aphids
- Mites
- Powdery mildew
- Bitter pit
- Blossom blast
- Apple maggot

Harvesting:

- Pears bear fruit in 3 to 5 years
- Fruit should be at least 2 inches in diameter before harvest
- Handle carefully as pears can bruise easily
- To test ripeness, cut a fruit open. Dark seeds indicate ripe fruit
- Harvest before fully ripe. Let pears ripen at room temperature

Storage:

- Keep pears in refrigerator for up to 1 week
- Pears will also store well in a cool, dark place in containers for 1 to 2 months
- Canning pears is another great way to increase shelf life

Friends:

- Alder
- Brambles
- Buckwheat
- Rye

Enemies:

- None

 Did you know? Putting your pears in a bowl with some bananas will help speed their ripening.

PLUM

Plum trees are a great gateway into fruit tree growing as they are less finicky than a lot of other fruits and do not require as much cultivation. This stone fruit has great antioxidant powers that can help alleviate cancer, diabetes, macular degeneration and more!

Popular Varieties:

- Satsuma
- Stanley
- Alderman
- Superior
- Underwood

Soil:

- Cultivate well-drained, moderately fertile soil

Planting:

- Plant at least two varieties of plum trees, as they will need to be cross-pollinated to produce fruit
- Find a sheltered position, such as a south or west facing spot out of the wind
- Remove plant from its pot and use shears to cut away any root bound soil
- Dig a hole that is a few inches deeper and wider than the root ball
- Space trees 20 to 25 feet apart
- Plums don't compete well with grass, so plant away from lawns

Light:

- Grow in full sun

Growing:

- Water heavily during the first week after planting to help establish roots
- Water regularly after the first week, soaking at the soil line
- Spread a thick layer of mulch to conserve moisture
- Shake limbs to thin or pinch off small, odd-shaped or overcrowded fruit before the pits harden. Leave 1 to 3 inches between small fruit and 3 to 5 inches between larger fruit
- Prune in early spring or mid-summer to avoid infection
- To protect winter injury, cover lower portion of the trunk in a tree wrap

Threats:

- Silver leaf disease
- Honey fungus
- Bacterial canker
- Pocket plum
- Japanese beetles
- Plum aphids
- Plum moth

Harvesting:

- Most plum trees will bear fruit 3 to 5 years after planting
- Plums turn color 20 to 30 days before harvest
- Pluck plums from the tree with some stem still attached. This will help plums store better
- If the skin of the fruit feels soft, plums are ripe and ready to harvest

Storage:

- Store plums in refrigerator for up to 2 weeks
- Plums are great for making jams and jellies
- This fruit also tastes great when frozen or dried as prunes

Enemies:

- Eggplant
- Pepper
- Raspberry
- Strawberry
- Tomato

Friends:

- Alder
- Brambles
- Buckwheat
- Rye
- Sorghum

 Did you know? China is the world's leading producer of plums, accounting for about half of world production.

RASPBERRIES

Raspberries don't travel well, which is why they're often considered a luxury fruit and come at a steep price in the supermarket. However, growing your own is extremely simple, as they're also the hardest bramble fruit. These perennial plants can bear a bountiful harvest indefinitely when cared for properly.

Popular Varieties:

- Canby
- Heritage
- Fallgold
- Plainsman

Soil:

- Cultivate rich, well-drained soil
- Prepare soil a few weeks before planting with 2 inches of compost and aged manure
- Till soil well

Planting:

- Plant potted transplants in the spring after the last threat of frost
- Make sure to choose a location for your raspberries that is protected from the wind and not on soggy ground
- Soak roost for 2 hours in bucket of water before planting
- Space plants 2 to 3 feet apart in rows 8 feet apart
- If you have chosen a climbing variety, provide a trellis, cage or fence for your raspberry plants to grow on
- Dig a large enough hole so that roots will fit without bending

Light:

- Grow in full sun

Growing:

- Ensure that there is a thick layer of mulch surrounding plants at all times
- Water 1 inch per week. Regular watering is better than deep soaking
- Prune shoots as they arise so that the main raspberry bush can receive full nutrients
- After harvest or in spring, cut out thin, weak or spindly canes and ones that have finished bearing fruit

Threats:

- Spider mites
- Japanese beetles
- Rabbits
- Powdery mildew
- Cane borers

Harvesting:

- When berries slide off easily without pressure, they are ripe
- Harvest into shallow containers to avoid crushing fruit

Storage:

- Freeze within 2 days of harvesting by spreading out on cookie sheet and sticking in freezer
- Store in heavy freezer bags once solid
- Keep in plastic bag in refrigerator for 4 to 7 days

Friends:

- Beans
- Peas
- Garlic
- Rue
- Tansy

Enemies:

- Nightshade

Did you know? If you are feeling a little lethargic, snacking on a handful of raspberries can perk you up. They are rich in manganese, a trace mineral that aids the body in converting fats and protein to energy.

STRAWBERRIES

Perennial strawberry plants are lauded among garden-growers, and with good reason! This delicious fruit can make any dessert better, or top toast or pancakes for a breakfast treat. Strawberries are inexpensive plants and relatively resistant to inclement weather conditions.

Popular Varieties:

- Northeaster
- Sable
- Primetime
- Cardinal
- Camarosa

Soil:

- Cultivate sandy-loamy soil
- Work in compost or aged manure a few months before planting
- Ensure that soil is well drained, plant in raised beds if necessary

Planting:

- Plant strawberries from nursery plants as soon as the ground can be worked in early spring
- As strawberries are sprawling plants, they need sufficient room to spread their runners
- Makes holes deep and wide enough to cover entire root system
- Gently refill hole with loose soil
- Space 20 inches apart in rows 4 inches apart
- You can also use a hill system to contain strawberry runners. Space plants 1 foot apart in rows, with 2 to 3 feet between rows
- Remove every runner to ensure that each plant begins forming a separate hill. This will allow for a more bountiful crop due to proper air circulation and light

Light:

- Grow in full sun

Growing:

- Lay down a thick layer of straw mulch to help suppress weeds. Hand-pull any that poke through
- Pick off blossoms in the first year to prevent fruit growth. This will allow plants to put more energy into developing strong root systems
- Water plants 1 inch per week during growing season
- Once ground has frozen, cover plants with fresh straw to protect them
- Remove mulch from plants in early spring to allow ground to warm up

Threats:

- Gray mold
- Powdery mildew
- Japanese beetles
- Spider mites
- Slugs

Harvesting:

- Harvest by pinching the stem to sever it
- Check plants every other day as strawberries mature quickly. Berries should be bright red and have a sweet taste
- Always harvest all ripe or malformed berries to prevent disease spread

Storage:

- Store unwashed berries in refrigerator for up to 5 days
- Freeze strawberries in airtight bag or container for as long as desired

Friends:

- Bush beans
- Lettuce
- Onion
- Sage
- Spinach

Enemies:

- Brassicas

 Did you know? Strawberries are the only fruit that show their seeds on the outside.

"A garden requires patient labor and attention. Plants do not grow merely to satisfy ambitions or to fulfill good intentions. They thrive because someone expended effort on them. "

— Liberty Hyde Bailey

Self Sufficiency is Possible For All

Whether you live on a large piece of land or in an urban setting, it is possible to grow your own food and provide for your family. It is my sincerest hope that this book has not only been a great informational and educational experience, but that it has also inspired you to take the first step towards being sustainable. As you spend time growing your own food, not only will you be healthier, but the skills that you learn in the process — and the skills you impart to your children — will be invaluable.

We never know what tomorrow will bring, or what challenges we will be faced with individually, as a community, as a country or even a world. It has always been my feeling that we should not take our industrial food system too seriously. It is overly complicated, marred by politics and corporations that are susceptible to more than you can imagine. I would much rather depend on myself and the good earth for as much as possible.

My desire for you is that your harvest be bountiful and your heart always be happy for the provision that comes from getting your hands dirty!

"God Almighty first planted a garden.
And indeed, it is the purest of human pleasures. "

— Francis Bacon

This page intentionally left blank.